MILLENNIAL MANIFESTO

AN ACTIVIST HANDBOOK BY, FOR, AND ABOUT
THE MILLENNIAL GENERATION.

Including:

- ✓ *Twelve Steps to Youth Activism*
- ✓ *A Guide to Millennial Generation Politics*
- ✓ *A Roadmap to the March Across America*
- ✓ *A Blueprint for the National Youth Platform*
- ✓ *And What to Expect on Election Day 2004*

By:

Scott Beale with Abeer B. Abdalla
Founders of Millennial Politics.com

With Foreword By:
William Strauss and Neil Howe
*Authors of Generations, Fourth Turning
and Millennials Rising*

December 2003, Second Print

DEDICATED TO YOUTH ACTIVISTS EVERYWHERE,

to anyone who has ever believed in a voice, who believes
in monumental change for themselves and our world.
This is dedicated to all those with homemade soapboxes
and to anyone looking to learn how to create their own.
This is for dreamers, for doers, and for anyone who
believes that the only "ism" that counts is ACTIVism.

10% of the proceeds from this book will support non-profits that, in turn, support youth activism. Including Youth Venture, Youth Vote, Mobilizing America's Youth, United Leaders, the National Youth Rights Association, and the 2100 Fund.

SPREAD THE WORD

Millennial Manifesto is available at one-third off the cover price for orders of ten or more books. Use this book as a fundraising tool for a good cause. Use it in classrooms or for summer readings. Start a book club. Give it as a gift. Spread the good news about our generation.

FOR MORE INFORMATION, GO TO WWW.MILLENNIALPOLITICS.COM

Possible Library of Congress Cataloging-in-Publication Data
Beale, John Scott, 1976 –
Abdalla, Abeer B., 1981 –
The Millennial Manifesto is a guide to youth activism, volunteerism and service, as well as the story of how the politics of the Millennial Generation will change America. / by Scott Beale with Abeer B. Abdalla.   Includes index and bibliographical references.
Summary: Provides a guide on how to be a youth activist as well as an overview of the political priorities of Americans born after 1975.
ISBN# 1-5919-6421-0

Cover Design by fifteen-year-old Samuel Thomas, & by Tracy Mann.
Printed in Collierville, TN

MILLENNIAL MANIFESTO
ENDORSEMENTS

Dozens of organizations, youth leaders, youth advocates, elected officials, political leaders, and likeminded authors have endorsed the following statement:

"We endorse the Millennial Manifesto: Youth Activist Handbook as a powerful tool to educate and motivate young people about youth activism and generational politics.

While we may not agree with every stance taken in this book, we believe that these issues are important and need to be addressed by this generation."

To see the list of endorsements, please go to:
www.millennialpolitics.com/endorsements

Be sure to read the back cover and back pages for more critical praise of *Millennial Manifesto*!

TABLE OF CONTENTS

FOREWORD
BY NEIL HOWE AND WILLIAM STRAUSS

ABOUT HOWE AND STRAUSS

Neil Howe and William Strauss are historians and the best selling authors of Generations (1991), 13th Gen (1993), The Fourth Turning (1997), and Millennials Rising (2000). They write and lecture frequently on generational issues. They host active discussions with readers (at millennialsrising.com and fourthturning.com). They are among the leading experts in America about generational theory, especially the rising Millennial Generation.

Neil Howe is also an economist, demographer, and frequent media commentator on fiscal policy, retirement, and global aging. Howe is a senior advisor to the Concord Coalition and senior policy advisor to the Blackstone Group.

William Strauss is also a playwright, theatrical director, and entertainer. He is the co-founder and director of the Capitol Steps, a professional satirical troupe that has performed over 5,000 shows.

FOREWORD

In today's America, too many people assume that young people always and everywhere have little interest in politics—that they have no agenda, that their preferences are easy to manipulate, and that unless you make it "fun," they won't pay attention. This is wrong. There is nothing intrinsic about the human lifecycle, or about politics, that dictates that the old must be more politically powerful than the young.

The past two decades have indeed revealed a political disinterest, and weakness, in the most recent batch of young people, alias Generation X. The fact that they vote lightly is well documented. Their high-priority issues tend toward the personal. One consequence is that, from childhood to the brink of middle age, Gen Xers have fared poorly whenever politicians get together to divvy up resources. Look at the tax code. Look at Social Security. Look at health care or housing or welfare—everywhere you turn, you see institutions disfavoring whatever age bracket Gen X happens to occupy at the time.

How short our memories are. Around the time the first Gen Xers were born—the early 1960s—a common complaint was about the powerlessness of old people. By far the most politically muscular generation was in midlife, the "G.I. Generation" that had fought World War II, built the suburbs, and was building rockets aimed at the moon (and Vietnam). When they were young adults, back in the 1930s, young adults had the most political power. They cast the largest generational vote—over 80 percent—ever measured (for FDR). They were the prime beneficiaries of the New Deal.

Look at the movies of the 1930s and see how they depicted young people—as civically engaged, smart, determined, earnest activists, often in uniform. The leading teen movie of their time, *Babes in Arms*, has a big Busby Berkeley finale, with dozens of business-suited teenagers and collegians descending the steps of the U.S. Capitol, singing "here we go a-marching, your nation's future presidents." And, in the end, they *did* produce more presidents than any other generation in U.S. history. From youth to old age, the G.I. Generation was a political powerhouse.

The way history works, a new such generation appears whenever an old such generation expires. Junior citizens step in to fill the role just vacated by senior citizens.

Enter the Millennials.

Today's collegians and high school students, and the kids coming along after them, show every sign of being intensely interested in politics. We've forecast for some time that they will vote heavily when the time comes. And even before they can vote in a number that is likely to be decisive nationally (probably in the 2010s), their sheer energy and activism as volunteers—coming to rallies putting up signs, canvassing neighborhoods, operating phone- and internet-banks—will spell the difference between victory and defeat for many a candidate.

In their emerging mindset, politics is mainstream and serious, not just for policy wonks or Saturday Night Live joke-fests. They are coming of age poised to launch major political movements, to propel candidacies, to set *and achieve* a new youth-driven agenda. There is good news, and some worrisome news, for both political parties. On the whole, their economic agenda may please Democrats more than Republicans, their social and cultural agenda the other way around. They will adhere less willingly to anti-war positions than their recent predecessors in youth (that's already been true, in Afghanistan and Iraq), and will be prepared to sacrifice some personal freedoms for a greater sense of security (witness the many young voices in favor of a *universal* national youth service program).

In many ways—most ways—their agenda has yet to take shape. It will be driven in part by the years in which they've grown up, but also in part by events that have yet to happen. The 9/11 and Columbine tragedies have already influenced their politics in fundamental ways, but cannot alone explain their new sense of cohesion, specialness, optimism, and faith in the capacity of civic institutions to do important work.

Millennials are not X, not even close, a fact that is often lost on Hollywood these days. Nor are they some "Gen Y" extension of Gen X. Not even close—which is one reason we've encountered nearly no one currently under age 21 who uses or even likes that term. While they get along with their parents (and other adults) better than any other youths in the history of polling, they are not at all "echo Boomers." It's more correct to call Millennials *anti*-Boomers, history's correctives for the "mistakes" they perceive that their parents are making.

We, and most others, define the Millennial cutting edge as starting with babies born in the early 1980s. Scott and Abeer set the initial Millennial boundary five years earlier than we do, which is in some ways an important difference. In our view, the political attitudes and behaviors of Americans born in the late 1970s have several aspects of Gen X. But in at least one way, this five-year boundary difference is *not* important. Here again, history is a useful guide.

Recall how, in the 1960s, so many of the Boomer movements were set in motion by somewhat older (Silent) generation activists. Kicking off the '60s-era youth movement was an organization called Students for a Democratic Society (SDS), whose founding document, the Port Huron Statement, had no Boomer coauthors. The Chicago Seven were all born before 1943—as were Stokely Carmichael, Bob Dylan, Jerry Rubin, Gloria Steinem, Joan Baez, Abbie Hoffman, Huey Newton, and Bobby Seale. Throughout the Vietnam War, the leaders of anti-war and pro-civil rights "youth" were people in their mid- to late-twenties. Boomers followed many (though not all) of the paths they laid—or, at least, had plenty of dorm-room arguments over them. By the 1970s, those movements, or what remained of them, became fully Boomer.

We expect that the same will happen in the years ahead, as the young edge of Gen X mentors the new movements of this Millennial Generation. At some point, probably around 2010, we'll hear and see this new cadre of youth speak, and act, on its own.

What Scott and Abeer have done, here, is to provide Millennials with a very thought-provoking initial blueprint. We agree with much of what they're saying, and where we do not, the authors provide an excellent starting point for good conversations. We find their how-tos on civic activism to be particularly helpful.

Throughout this book, the particulars matter less than the authors' core point, with which we totally concur. Something new is about to break out, in the world of politics, from this Millennial Generation. Something large. Something powerful. America will be the better for it.

William Strauss and Neil Howe
(co-authors of *Generations, 13th-Gen, The Fourth Turning,* and *Millennials Rising*)

PART ONE:

THE MOVEMENT

"We are the generation we have been waiting for!"
– *Marc Kielburger*, *Millennial Founder of Leaders Today.*

INTRODUCTION

A Better World is Possible

For far too long, young Americans have been overlooked, undervalued, and misunderstood. An entire generation has been growing up shackled by the stereotypes of generations past and the socially acceptable discrimination against youth. But not anymore. Instead, we are standing up to declare our generational identity, affirm our self-worth, proclaim what issues we care about, and decide in what direction we are taking this country. We are proud members of the Millennial Generation and this is our story.

The Millennial Generation

Americans born between 1976 and 1996 are the next great generation in our country's history.[1] We are not Generation X,[2] and Generation Y fails to capture our uniqueness as the first generation to come of age in the new millennium. Some people call us the: DARE Generation, Hip Hop Generation, September 11 Generation, Net Generation, Sunshine Generation, and more. For this book, we prefer the name "The Millennial Generation" because, just as the year 2000 offered hope and promise for the future, so too does our generation. The turn of the millennium

---

[1] Among many reasons, we also chose 1976 because the last year of the decline in U.S. annual births. According to the *Census,* in 1977 the birth rate increased from under 3.2 million per year to over 4.2 million by 1990.
[2] We define Generation X as Americans born from 1961 to 1975. We refer to people in this generation as "Gen X."

represented advances in technology and a new global outlook that are our generation's reality. The year 2000 also brought to the forefront concerns about terrorist threats and technology run amuck. Fear and faith for the future, potential not yet met – this is our generation. We are Millennials.

Five significant influences and events differentiate Millennials from Gen Xers and, in doing so, shape our generation's identity. These five factors are (1) the end of the Cold War, (2) the Information Revolution, (3) the new economy, (4) our increasingly diverse society, and (5) the events of September 11, 2001.

The End of the Cold War

Millennials were thirteen years old or younger when the Berlin Wall came down and symbolically ended the Cold War. Unlike Gen Xers and Boomers[3] who feared the A-bomb while growing up and may have practiced nuclear war drills hidden underneath desks in school, Millennials never pictured where they would be on *The Day After*[4] the bomb fell. The end of the Cold War ushered in a "New World Order." Globalization flourished and previously closed countries opened their borders to tourists, trade, and their own internal conflicts. Multinational corporations and international organizations proliferated, as did our awareness of the people outside of the United States, beyond the two dimensional internationalism of a bi-polar world.

The Information Revolution

Millennials ranged from teenagers to infants in 1995 when the Internet changed the world.[5] As a result, most Millennials

---

[3] "Boomers" are members of the Baby Boom, or Boomer generation – Americans born from 1943-1960.

[4] *The Day After* was a made-for-TV movie about the day after nuclear war. Nearly every Gen Xer stayed up late to see this movie and regretted it for years to come.

[5] In Chapter Two we define why 1995 was such a critical year. Among other things it was the year that Mosaic was created, immediately leading to the program Netscape that allowed users to "surf the web."

don't use phone books, foldable maps, or heavy dictionaries – we go online for just about everything. Even the cell phone savvy teenagers of today will frequently IM (instant message) more often than they speed dial, and many of us read online presses as our primary source of "print" news. The Information Revolution has empowered us unlike any other generation in the history of the United States. The web enables us to organize our thoughts with issue-oriented or personality-reflecting web pages. Online discussion boards, newsletters, and email allow us to meet other like-minded individuals and learn from their experiences. Through the web, activists organize from Los Angeles to New York City and find solidarity with people overseas. In short, the Internet has turned traditional power structures upside-down, empowering students to teach their teachers, and kids to show their parents the way. Young, ambitious activists are molding a new era in history.

The New Economy

The leading Millennials' formative years coincided with the economic boom of the 1990s. Despite the recent economic downturn, many Millennials have grown up and benefited from a strong American economy. According to a KidsPeace report, "'Significantly, the word crisis does not appear to be in the teen lexicon.' The Cold War is over. And even if the economy is slowing and the NASDAQ has a bad year, the Internet keeps getting faster and cell phones cheaper."[6] Furthermore, the new American economy, whether up or down, remains unmatched globally. Growing up in the 80s, Gen Xers read about how Tokyo would replace New York City, but Millennials never had reason to doubt our nation's economic dominance.

However, despite our nation's wealth far too many Millennials have grown up in poverty and with lack of

---

[6] Strauss and Howe, <u>Millennials Go To College</u>, p. 33. (a.k.a *Millennials2College*)

opportunities. And at the turn of the millennium, we witnessed our federal budget change from record surpluses to record debts. "Joblessness is at a nine-year high of 6.1 percent, ... and an ABC News headline in May 2003 screamed, 'With No Jobs, 60% of Class of 2003 Moving Back With Parents."[7] In the summer of 2003, the Children's Defense Fund (CDF) reported that teen joblessness hit a 55 year high of 59.1 percent. Among Black and Hispanic teens the rate was even higher. Increasingly, we are beginning to wonder if our parents have improved upon a financially strong country they inherited from our grandparents or if they are stealing from our generation and creating a fiscally hollow nation by borrowing from their kids.

An Increasingly Diverse Society

Millennials have been shaped by an age of multiethnic Benetton commercials, open sexuality on television, and two decades of politically correct language. The 1990s witnessed a decade of liberalized immigration laws, and the year 2000 ushered in the first census accounting for multiracial children. We believe that love is color-blind.[8]

Diversity is no longer defined only by skin color alone. Young people today are more open, than other generations, to individuals with non-traditional sexual orientations.[9] Millennials have a rising awareness of the contributions that individuals with disabilities can make to society, especially when armed with new technologies. We also believe that feminism and affirmative action achieved important progress in the 20th century and now need a 21st century update.

---

[7] Weiner, Robert and Amy Rieth. "The Dwindling Youth Vote: Where Will It Be In 2004?" *The Christian Science Monitor*, 06/23/03.

[8] According to a 1999 youth poll on react.com 82% agreed that "Love is color-blind." Data from *Millennials2College*, p. 24.

[9] For example, the 2002 UCLA/HERI survey found that a record high 57.9% of freshmen believe that same sex couples should have the right to legal marital status, nearly a 2% increase from last year. And less than 25% believe the U.S. should enact laws prohibiting homosexual relationships.

Despite social advances, race does matter and many youth of color deal with racism on a daily basis. We are not free of bias; however, in our actions and in words, our generation is growing up committed to making progress to end discrimination of all types in our society.

The Events of September 11th

Our generation was raised to believe that we could do anything. Politics, technology, economy, and the society evolved to create seemingly endless opportunity, especially for younger Americans. We all thought we were invincible. Then the World Trade Center towers fell.

Our innocence was lost on September 11, 2001, the first day of the *Fourth Turning*[10] in American history. The activists of our generation found deeper meaning to our work than we have ever imagined; the apathetic among us found it harder to sit on the sidelines; and those of who were not quite activist, and certainly not apathetic, felt called to action. Unlike any conflict we had studied in our history books, terrorism interrupted our childhood.

Some of the American responses to these attacks also gave cause for concern. Much like when we first learned our parents were not perfect, we learned that the government could make mistakes in the name of freedom. Many of us feared the erosion of civil liberties,[11] and First Amendment rights appeared out the window as media outlets were quieted upon questioning the government. We wanted the government to protect us, but were not quite sure how to find comfort in a confused world.

---

[10] The Fourth Turning is a book and a concept by Strauss and Howe about generations and cycles in American History. There is more information about this important concept at the back of the book and online at: fourthturning.com.

[11] "81% of college students agree that the government should take steps to prevent additional acts of terrorism but not if those steps would affect some of your basic civil liberties such as personal privacy or free speech (62% of the general population feels this way)." According to Schneiders / Della Volpe / Schulman, "Campus Kids: The New Swing Voter." Harvard University, IOP Spring Survey, 5/21/03, p. 7. (a.k.a *CampusKids*)

Dumbfounded, we watched our nation's Republican leadership ignore some of the virtues of our government system that are worth defending.[12] We then turned to the Democrats and found either eager conspirators selling out our democracy or liberal peace-lovers who weren't willing to fight for our nation. Our generation stood helpless, confused, alone, and in the middle. At age 25 and younger we knew we would be fighting the upcoming war. We feared the draft. Our imaginations ran wild and for the first time we all lived with nightmares and uncertainty.

Every generation has a moment in time when a common experience bonds them together. For the members of the Millennial Generation, September 11, 2001, marked that defining moment. The last birth year of the Millennial Generation is 1996, since people born after that date may not remember where they were on the 11th. All Millennials will remember 9-11, even the five- and six-year-olds whose parents suddenly had to explain the unimaginable.

Who Are We to Write Millennial Manifesto

No one or two people could possibly be qualified to speak for an entire generation, especially one as diverse as the Millennials. Our bios are in the back of the book, but let us tell you quickly who we are.

Abeer Abdalla on Scott Beale

Scott is a youth activist and a youth advocate with ten years of experience. A fiercely proud Delawarean and Georgetown University graduate, Scott has been involved in registering thousands of young people to vote and helping elect Millennials to public office. He has a deep understanding of politics and has worked on every level of government (local, state, national, and

---

[12] According to many, The Patriot Act comes dangerously close to unconstitutionally infringing on individuals' right to privacy and allows the government to detain aliens in secret who they deem to be a threat to national security.

international), including in the White House with President Clinton and organizing elections in Bosnia. He has an inside-the-beltway (a.k.a. from Washington, D.C.) perspective of how the system is holding young people back and has been a participant and witness to hundreds of rallies and marches in the city. Even though we don't always agree, he defends the progressive point of view well and believes in our generation. He currently works at a non-profit called Youth Venture that supports Millennial activists all over the country and is attending graduate school at the University of Delaware. Scott is a marathon runner who never sleeps and he is a passionate spokesperson for youth activism and our generation.

Scott Beale on Abeer Abdalla

When I did a national search for a coauthor to help me with this book, Abeer described herself as a "vivacious, Arab-American, Republican female who believes in the power and potential of our generation." Abeer is a great foil to my Democratic point of view. Moonlighting for various organizations in Orlando, Florida, she can be found wherever Republican politics are hot. She has accumulated a great deal of activist experience after having worked in Boston with Service Vote 2000 and on a number of Republican campaigns over the last six years. Whether it is national organizations like the College Republicans, the Young Republicans, the National Federation of Republican Woman, or the League of Women Voters, she is passionate about the media and making sure our generation's voice is heard. Abeer and I don't agree on everything and we run in completely different circles. Abeer's variety of political affiliations from the National Rifle Association (NRA) to the American Civil Liberties Union (ACLU) is proof that our generation is not easily compartmentalized into traditional political boxes. Working together (and with the support of literally hundreds of other young leaders) we have tried to write a book that describes the majority of the generation, even if it is not entirely accurate for any one person.

A New Generation is on the Rise

Welcome to the Millennial Generation! We are a dynamic, diverse, digital generation that is changing the world. We are self-confident, group-oriented, and internationally aware.[13] We are just now beginning to get organized, and our generational identity is being formed. Our generation, the Millennials, is still young, but the roadmap is clear. By examining our political activity, it becomes obvious where we are taking this country and how soon we will be there. In the short period of time we have been alive, Millennials received so much from this country and we have an incredible opportunity and fundamental responsibility to give back much more.

We have worked hard to make Millennial Manifesto an introduction to our generation. If you're a Millennial, this book is written for you and it will detail for you some of the activism that exists in our generation as well as some of the activists shaping it. If you're not a Millennial, then this Millennial Manifesto will introduce you to our world, which is being overlooked by the evening news and the national papers. This book documents our political priorities, profiles some young leaders, and provides a roadmap for aspiring activists. This book also previews what's to come in 2004, including the Presidential Election and the March Across America. The accompanying website MillennialPolitics.com is full of facts and figures that supplement this book.

We've researched this book for over five years and received help from hundreds of Millennials (see the story at the end of the

---

[13] Don Tapscott, author of Growing Up Digital, describes Millennials as having a "very strong sense of the common good and of collective social and civic responsibility." From Howe and Strauss, Millennials Rising, p. 231.

book). While none of us alone can possibly claim to represent the entire generation, we have tried to briefly present the attitudes and behaviors of our peers. Although just a 'sampler,' this book will give you a good taste of where a majority of youth stands today, and where we are going tomorrow.

However, we know we don't have all the answers. We encourage your feedback. We plan on updating and republishing the book, so add your voice and make the next edition even more timely and representative. Go online to millennialpolitics.com. Let us know what you think, and find out how you can get involved.

Our generation has no excuse not to be engaged and work for social change. As you are about to read, there are many pressing issues that demand the creative, capable hands, and minds of the Millennials. We must not sit idly by and listen to the band play on as our nation sinks, unable to overcome partisan rhetoric and a public turned off to our failing democracy. We will not be passive participants in our nation's politics; it is time for us to make ourselves be heard!

"As a generation, we have many problems to deal with. We embrace our identity, we are a multi-tendency and cross-cultural group of citizens untangling problems that, for the first time in history, are inseparable from the global critique ... We will be criticized for a 'lack of focus,' for being whiners, and social critics from movements past will scratch their heads as we unite for political prisoners on Monday, dispossessed indigenous persons on Tuesday, workers' rights on Wednesdays and spend the rest of the week quietly reading Howard Zinn to grade school kids. But unlike our predecessors, we will not sell out after the 'revolution.' We were sold out in the cradle, and now we're expected to counter the most widespread, pervasive and well-founded monolith that mankind has ever seen. We were raised to believe that the monolith was as the world is. It is all that there ever has been. When we realized that a good portion of humanity is being crushed beneath it we didn't know where to begin chipping away. Service is a small hammer. By itself it can send small chips flying. Politics acts like a chisel. To its own, it can gouge the perfect surface. Together, with our hard work and inspiration, the hammer and chisel begin to carve something new, less perfect, and more humane."[1]

Fabricio Rodriguez
Mesa Community College
Wingspread Summit Participant

"The State of the Movement is that almost no one in the Movement, let alone anyone outside of it, has any idea how much is going on." — *William Upski Wimsatt*[14]

1

MILLENNIAL REVOLUTION

We are a new generation. We are the 77 million Americans who were born during or after 1976. Don't believe the hype that we are apolitical, apathetic, individualistic, violent, and disengaged. We are a self-confident, group-oriented, internationally aware, technologically savvy, civic minded, well-educated and upbeat generation that is going to shape (and already is shaping) the politics of the 21st century. We've grown up in an era free of fear, yet we lost our childhood innocence on September 11, 2001. The civic fabric of our country, so carefully cherished for by our forefathers, has been worn thin by decades of neglect. No longer are we a "nation at risk"[15] because of the behaviors of our youth; indeed, we are a nation at risk because of the hypocrisy of our parents and new threats from foreign lands.

We have many concerns about the problems in our world, most notably:

- International Terrorism & Domestic Xenophobia
- Lack of Civic Participation & Personal Responsibility
- Economic, Racial & Educational Disparities
- Environmental Neglect, and
- Cultural Liberalism

---

[14] Future 500. Active Element Foundation, p. 3. (a.k.a. *Future500*)
[15] "A Nation At Risk" is an April 1983 report from the National Commission on Excellence in Education.

Those of us who are liberal are upset with eight years of missed opportunities for the Democratic Party, and the rest of us conservatives look to our elder Republican leaders and wonder if anything will ever change. But it will change, because we are going to alter the course of history by addressing these issues and more. We will not accept one in seven voters turning out for Congressional elections. We will not stand by and watch selfish CEOs avoid corporate responsibility. We will not condone politicians taking money from teachers' unions and claiming to be reforming education. We will not let trial lawyers hijack our judicial system. We will not watch a nation of pseudo-environmentalists paint their SUVs green and celebrate Earth Day by drinking champagne out of Styrofoam cups. We will not accept Hollywood's negative portrayal of youth. Unlike our older Gen X siblings, we've had enough of it all.

Thomas Jefferson said our country would occasionally benefit from a revolutionary generation. Wake up America, a new day is dawning.

Why Is This Book Important?

Why should we spend any time reading about our generation since everything that we have ever read up until today indicates: that we don't vote, don't know what's going on, and don't care? It is important because fewer voters mean more elite and extreme voters leading to policy that does not reflect average citizens, especially our generation. It is important because if the cancer of civic disengagement continues, then our democracy will be left to atrophy in the hospital bed, an old nation wondering why its grandchildren are not taking care of its glorious traditions. It is important because generations, like individuals, rise or fall to whatever expectations are placed on them. And with the incredible political and technological advancements in the world, that our generation has seen, there are no excuses for low expectations.

This book is important because there are those who do not want to see young people seize power. They do not want us to ask questions; they do not want us to vote; and they certainly do not want us to be active. Many in our generation are being locked up in jails and psychiatric institutions for reasons ranging from drug use to problems with authority. Alex Asch, a sixteen-year-old student at the Institute for Social Ecology, was diagnosed with having Oppositional Defiance Order and locked up until he turns eighteen. Some of the symptoms of this disorder include often losing one's temper, arguing with adults, and actively defying or refusing to comply with adults' requests. Alex may be a liberal activist, but he is not crazy for wanting to make the world a better place. He would be crazy not to.[16]

A New Era

Since the early 1980s the country has developed a love affair with youth (as least those who are not activists). Millennials have neither been neglected nor have suffered like previous generations, especially in comparison to Generation X. The nuclear family structure may have changed, but our parents or guardians still make sure that we do our work in school and are signed up for the local soccer teams. Young girls have encountered role models unlike previous generations of women. These women have excelled in the classroom, on the sports fields, and in the boardrooms. Young women have many reasons today to be self-confident. We [young women] were encouraged, in fact pressured, to do well in school and record numbers of us have gone on to college and have become the best-educated generation in history.[17]

As youths, we were introduced to the Internet and all the educational and entertainment value of the Information

---

[16] Shukaitis, Stevphen. "Just Call Them Crazy." *WireTap*, 06/12/03. See: wiretapmag.org/story.html?StoryID=16151 Viewed on 6/21/03.
[17] Schneider, Barbara and David Stevenson. Ambitious Generation, p. 215. See also supporting facts in Chapter Nine.

Revolution. Even before we were old enough to drive, we had access to more information than the best educated people of previous generations. This, along with the end of the Cold War and the internationalism of the 1990s, has opened up previously unknown possibilities for us. Just like the international organization *Doctors Without Borders*, we are a generation that transcends boundaries, crossing the lines of race, ethnicity, and nationality with an ease that is often taken for granted.

We've grown up less affiliated with the traditional political parties than previous generations. We saw Ross Perot make a credible run for the Presidency; we cheered as Jesse Ventura surprised the nation by motivating the disinterested to turn out on Election Day; we attended Ralph Nader's "super" rallies and listened to him preach a new brand of politics; we observed Senator Jeffords turn his back on his party and change the political balance of power overnight. We care more about issues than party or personality.[18] We are too savvy to turn out and vote blindly for parties that do not listen to us.

As independent-minded youth with a wide variety of political beliefs, the traditional parties and the media establishment have chosen to label us disinterested and have not devoted the energy to educate or motivate us to get involved. We are seen as a gamble. Why motivate eighteen-year-olds to register and try to get them to the polls on Election Day if they may not pull the lever that keeps you, the elected party, in power? Political parties have myopically written off

> **Youth Activism Resource:**
> **Youth Action Net**
> Organized by the International Youth Foundation, Youth Action Net seeks to connect, inspire, and nurture young leaders. Its discussion forums connect youth from around the world to educate, inspire, and empower each other. Youth Action Net also provides money to youth to promote social change.
> www.youthactionnet.org

---

[18] *TrustMatters*, p. 36.

youth to solidify their electoral strength with the older Americans. No wonder Generation X said 'no thank you' to the process. This cycle of neglect needs to change and we've come to realize that the establishment is not going to change it. We cannot wait around for politicians to start asking us what we want. We need to stand up and make our voices heard.

Opportunity to Revolt

In any given Presidential election, approximately half of the country votes. In fact, with voters eighteen to twenty-four, turnout was about thirty-two percent in the last two Presidential elections. This means that on that special Tuesday in November, two out of every three Millennials of voting age decided that it was not worth spending five minutes to decide who will run the country for the next four years. Therefore, especially for young people, Presidential elections are decided by a very small number of votes. In the 2000 Presidential race, even in states that were not labeled "battleground states," victory could have swung to a different candidate had just a small percentage of the non-voters changed their mind and decided to vote on Election Day.

We, as a generation, also have a significant ability to decide elections because we are a nonaligned group. According to Dan Glickman, Director of Harvard University's Institute of Politics and a former US Cabinet Secretary and member of Congress, "'Campus Kids' can be the key swing group of the 2004 elections if the campaigns and candidates for office properly engage them."[19] Our generation can be the swing voters in close elections because we are divided evenly on party affiliation: "29 percent Democrats, 26 percent Republicans, and 41 percent Independents."[20]

---

[19] *CampusKids.*
[20] *CampusKids.*

Millennial Candidates

From big elections to small elections, we can make the difference. Certainly there are 500 Millennials who could have voted in Florida to change the outcome of the 2000 Presidential Election. In some local elections we are already making the difference, especially when another member of our generation runs for office. Meet Jeffrey Dunkel and Christopher Portman, two Millennials from Pennsylvania. They each ran for mayor in their respective towns in 2002 – and won![21]

Pennsylvania also has two Millennial state representatives: Jeff Coleman (age 27) and David Reed (age 25). According to Jeff, "We have record numbers of 18- to 24-year-olds registering to vote in our legislative districts ... We live in western Pennsylvania, which is kind of soured and cynical about the political process. This is a hard-hit region economically. Having a couple of young people in public office has inspired folks that had been away from the ballot box for a few years. It also sends a message to young citizens that it's OK, that politics and public service is noble."[22]

The youngest legislator in the nation lives in Ohio. Derrick Seaver was elected to the Ohio State Legislature at age eighteen when he was still in high school. He is twenty-one now and considered a seasoned representative and a "boy wonder"[23] according to his colleague, Ohio State Representative Charles Wilson.

The youngest candidate for Congress in 2004 might be Samara Barend. If successful at twenty-six years old, then she will be the youngest-ever woman elected to Congress. This dynamic young leader is a graduate of University of Pennsylvania and Harvard's Kennedy School. A runner active in

---

[21] See: youthnoise.com/site/CDA/CDA_Page/0,1004,522,00.html. Viewed on 6/1/03.
[22] Murphy, Kathleen. *Ohio Lawmaker Is Dean Of Kiddie Caucus, Stateline.org,* 05/06/03 stateline.org/story.do?storyId=303569. Viewed on 06/01/03.
[23] Murphy, Kathleen. Ibid.

Democratic politics who has even started a non-profit to help kids with mental illness, Samara is a rising star in the Millennial Generation. From small Pennsylvania towns to large states like New York, dozens of Millennials are beginning to make themselves noticed by running for public office. Soon there will be hundreds.

Case Study Campaign Georgetown

At Georgetown University, a dozen students who attended the Youth Vote '96 conference returned to school inspired to make a difference with campus – community relations. The students decided to earn their own representation in the local government. By November, 1000 students were registered to vote and two students were on the ballot for the eight-member Advisory Neighborhood Commission. On Election Day, over ninety percent of registered students turned out to vote and both young candidates won their election. One of them, Rebecca Sinderbrand, won by just five votes. These Millennials were beginning to flex their generational muscles and they were not alone.

> **Youth Activist Step #1**
> *Get Upset About An Issue*
> Students were upset about the way the community was treating them so they were inspired to take action.

Political Scandal

Unfortunately, the media chooses to ignore our activism and focuses on our flaws. Regretfully, the most famous political Millennial is Monica Lewinsky. Her improper relationship triggered a chain of events that led to the December 19, 1998 vote to impeach of President Clinton. However, unlike Watergate, Vietnam, or Iran-Contra, today's controversies do not directly undermine our faith in government. President Clinton's faults do not make us doubt the entire system, but rather they raise questions about his moral leadership. We are skeptical that politicians are honest, not that the system is corrupt. It is a subtle, but significant difference. If you think the system is flawed, you don't participate; but if you think the people are flawed, it encourages you to get involved.

Millennial Turnout

Despite some exciting candidates and positive changes in the law, we are not yet a generation of voters. There is, however, some recent evidence suggesting what it will take to turn more of us out to vote. Some of us remember Ross Perot's campaign and how he excited many of us who were previously disillusioned with politics. Perot's straightforward, businesslike approach to the government and the federal budget appealed to many of us, even if we weren't old enough to vote. Jesse Ventura's campaign for the Governor of Minnesota also illustrates this point. This former professional wrestler and actor mobilized the youth of Minnesota. Ventura's influence with the young, disaffected generation is undeniable – sixteen percent of the electorate was first-time voters who registered at the polls (not legal in all states). In addition, political leaders Ralph Nader and John McCain have each inspired many of us. Nader appealed to Millennials with his issue oriented, environmentally focused campaign, and McCain's leadership, honesty, and candor resonated with young voters. [24]

Our generation also should be voting at higher rates because of the affect of the motor-voter law. We are the first eighteen-year-olds able to register to vote when we updated our drivers' licenses. Fewer of us have to worry whether the paperwork is done, so we can show up easily on Election Day without being turned away from the polls. Furthermore, the motor-voter law made it easier for organizations to register Millennials even if we are not suburban kids getting permits for our new cars. Recent election legislation has rolled back some of the ease of voter

---

[24] The Campaign For Young Voters has a great deal of information about how candidates can reach young people. What Ventura, Nader and McCain were able to accomplish can be replicated with some simple approaches to Millennial voters. See: campaignyoungvoters.org

registration, but it is yet to be seen if it will negatively affect the young voter.

However, third party candidates and changes in voting laws have not yet done the trick as the voting decline continues within our generation. But, it won't take much to turn it around. A 2000 study by two Yale professors and the Youth Vote Coalition showed that when a young person makes a nonpartisan motivational request to another young person to vote on Election Day, voter turnout jumps approximately eight percent higher than if that young person had not been contacted at all.[25] In 2002 this study was replicated with a larger sample size and turnout increased by 11 percent.[26] Especially with current voting rates (32% in 2000), this is a *revolutionary* jump in turnout.

Non-partisan, peer-to-peer (and youth-to-adult) 'get out the vote' efforts work wonders. In 2002, the youth-led group Freedom's Answer created a network of over 2,500 schools in a nationwide effort to set a record for voter turnout in a non-presidential election year. These students collected pledges from millions of adults and asked them to keep America strong in response to September 11, 2001. These Millennials, most of them not old enough to vote themselves, demonstrated that they were old enough to lead and contribute to the increased turnout in 2002.[27]

Another group that demonstrated the value of peer-to-peer get out the vote efforts is Vote for America. When piloted in Rhode Island during the 2000 elections, Vote for America raised turnout almost six percent for the general public and forty-one percent for Millennials.[28] Rebecca Lieberman, daughter of Senator Joe Lieberman, is the founder of this nonpartisan group that expanded to four states in 2002.

---

[25] Professor Donald Green and Associate Professor Alan Gerber.
[26] See civicyouth.org for more information.
[27] According to exit polls, turnout increased in 2002. Walsh, Edward. "Election Turnout Rose to 39.3%" *WashPost*, 11/8/02, p. A10.
[28] See: voteforamerica.org/who_we_are/ Viewed on 6/02/03.

We, as a generation, need to do more. We need to ask the government to make substantial changes such as passing sincere voting reform legislation that genuinely reduces the barriers to voter participation. We would be more empowered if same day voter registration, instant run-off voting, and free air time legislation (among others) were passed.[29] It also helps when more relevant information about candidates gets into the hands of young people. Project Vote Smart, the League of Women Voters and Mobilizing America's Youth are educating young people about candidates.

A Patriotic Generation

The political history of our generation is short and we certainly know there is much more to politics than voting. But we are a patriotic generation that passionately believes in our country. Take, for example, the experience of these Millennials from a few summers ago: In 2001, a group of high school students visiting the Jefferson Memorial became so filled with patriotic pride they spontaneously burst into singing the National Anthem. "It was an awesome feeling. You just thought, I am so blessed to be a part of this great country," said Kirsten Winston, a student in the group. However, that feeling did not last long. "We got to almost the very end and we were at the last stanza when the National Park Service asked us to stop," said Kirsten. A Park Ranger asked them to stop because according to a federal regulation, any time a group of twenty-six people or more gathers at a national monument and attracts an audience, it is considered a demonstration, which requires a permit. However, the students were ultimately vindicated; the National Parks Service apologized for the mistake and said that people won't be stopped from singing the National Anthem again.

---

[29] There are more reforms discussed in Chapter 10.

Unlike our Boomer parents, we will not revolt against the system, but instead stage a revolution from within the system. As the high school students from Freedom's Answer clearly stated, "We're sick of being cynical. We're sick of being ignored. We're scared at what will happen if we don't speak up."[30] Unlike the gray haired politicians and CEOs running this country, we'll be around for another fifty years and we want government policy to reflect that reality. The future remains uncertain, but our forecast indicates a Millennial Storm is on the way.

---

[30] Clayton, Zach, et. al. <u>Freedom's Answer</u>, p.145.

"Hollywood, wake up and smell the double mocha latte. Today's teens aren't Gen X. They're not like you. Not even close. And the kids coming along behind them, now in middle school, are even less like you." – *William Strauss and Neil Howe*[31]

2

RAISING GIANTS

We are growing up during dynamic times. The world is beginning to feel like a very small place – countries' borders are becoming more open, the global economy more interdependent, and the media more omnipresent. Since CNN started broadcasting in 1980, it has brought major, live news events simultaneously into homes around the world. Apple revolutionized the personal computer in 1984 and a decade later the Internet burst onto the scene. The revolutions of Gen X have become our reality.

Changes in technology, culture, and the media have been written about with such frequency that we almost take for granted how different the world was before the Information Revolution. Few adults can fully comprehend how different growing up is today than it was when they were young. The most important byproduct of the Information Revolution on the generation is the pervasive self-confidence that it brings to today's youth. There has always existed a certain idealism, a perhaps naïve desire to change the world, among youth, but for

---

[31] Strauss and Howe, "Teens Shun Youth Gross Out Movie Genre." *LATimes*, 7/15/01, Opinion Section, p. 1

the first time in history, technology actually makes such change possible.

Technology

According to T.J. Becker of the *Chicago Tribune*, "The greatest hallmark of the Millennium Generation is its comfort with technology. Although Generation Xers are computer savvy, Millennials are technologically precocious, growing up with a rattle in one hand and a mouse in the other."[32] When Gen Xers were still buying records and tapes, we were asking for CD players and video game systems with computer chips powerful enough to operate foreign countries' missile systems.[33] Most of us have never used a manual or even an electric typewriter. We apply to college using computer disks and keep photo albums with digital cameras. Millennials are pre-teens on cell phones and organized students using Palm Pilots.

Yet the most influential invention on our generation is not a hand-held device. It is the Internet. As Greg Miller from the *L.A. Times* puts it, "What truly separates them [Millennials] from other age groups – even from their older brothers and sisters – is that they entered college just as universities across the country were installing high-speed Internet lines in the dorms."[34] At UCLA they, "began offering high-speed access to all 6,500 on-campus residents in 1995."[35] By the spring semester of 1997, 95 percent of undergraduate university students across the country were using the Internet. The effects of these emerging technologies cannot be overstated. As Scott Sanders from Sightsound.com said, "We have this one generation where the

---

[32] Becker, T.J. "Enter, the Millennials." *ChiTrib*, 1/31/99, p. C1

[33] "Saddam Hussein bought as many as 4,000 of Sony's PlayStation and new high-tech PlayStation 2 game consoles, and may be using them to construct a sophisticated missile-guidance system." Rose, Alexander. "Iraq is armed … with PlayStation 2" *Chicago Sun-Times*, 12/27/00.

[34] Miller, Greg. "Ethernet is Changing Dorm Life." *LATimes*, 01/14/00. p. A1.

[35] Miller, Greg. Ibid

parents have no clue and the kids know nothing else. It's the biggest technological generation gap in history."[36]

Email distribution lists and web pages revolutionized student and grassroots organizing. In the fall semester of 1994, the University of Missouri-Rolla Student Council created the *Internet Headquarters for Student Governments*. This site connected student governments across the country – an idea that had been impractical only one year earlier. By offering inexpensive communication to an unlimited audience, the web offers both tremendous market possibilities and potential to organize that no previous generation has had available to them.

During the dot-com boom of the late 1990s, the Information Revolution has also transferred a great amount of potential wealth to some Millennials. In the late 90s, students graduated from college and rode the tech wave up, and then eventually down. Even high school kids got in on the act. Instead of babysitting and cutting grass to make money, fifteen-year-olds are presenting web design proposals to major businesses. D.A. Wallach is one such example. When he heard how much the "professional" web design companies were going to charge the company his mother works for, he put together their own business proposal and won the contract.[37]

The Information Revolution that began while the first Millennials were in college will have an even more profound impact on the younger members of the generation. At Dartmouth College in New Hampshire, every student has email on his/her desk all of the time. Students don't call across campus; they "blitz mail." At the Gateway High School in St. Louis, students read the news online rather than subscribing to a local paper. Many Millennials have turned off network T.V. and opt to inform and entertain themselves through the Internet. Even shopping is done online now as students purchase books,

---

[36] Miller, Greg. Ibid
[37] Interview with D.A. Wallach on July 10, 2001 by Scott Beale.

music, and clothes online rather than at the campus store. Unlike older generations who are adapting to new methods and norms established by the Internet, Millennials have grown up with this technology. Take a look at any teenager – they are as comfortable using the Internet as they are using a phone or driving a car. None of these inventions are considered new to us. We should also note that wealthier Americans have benefited from the Information Revolution at a greater level than poorer Americans. However, lower- and middle-class families have not been isolated from this revolution. As a whole, rich or poor, black or white, urban or rural, Americans born after 1975 have been shaped by the Internet more profoundly than those older than them. Just ask fifteen-year-old Kenny Wiggins, a public school student in Washington, D.C. His web design company continues to grow despite slower economic times. He didn't let age, race, or socio-economic class hold him back.[38]

Technology and Politics

This revolution is about more than just universities and the private sector; the government began to change too, and with this revolution a whole set of new political issues has arisen. The earliest political issues were about e-government, and bringing public schools and government up to speed with the growing Internet. Despite the initial expense, this happened quickly. By 1998, Delaware became the first state to wire every high school to the Internet, and other states soon followed.

After access, privacy became the most important political issue regarding new technology. Millennials became concerned with everything from credit card fraud to government exploitation of programs like "Carnivore" that allows the FBI access to commercial servers (do you want Uncle Sam reading your email?). In addition to privacy, the government has

---

[38] Kenny W. is a Youth Venturer who has worked with Scott Beale in Washington, DC.

struggled to regulate Information Age companies with Industrial Age laws. The AOL-Time Warner merger, the Microsoft monopoly case, and the Napster copyright case have all been thrown to the courts and debated in the public. Even free speech issues were raised as pornography proliferated on the Internet and kids learned how to make bombs, cheat on tests, and create fake IDs. Software to block these pages from teenage eyes rushed in, but sometimes this software prevented users on library computers to visit web sites like the American Cancer Society's.

In 1996, a group of teens in Seattle created a website called Peacefire to fight against Internet censorship and for First Amendment rights for people under eighteen on the Internet. This group does everything from working with the ACLU,

> **Youth Activism Resource:**
> **Rock The Vote (RTV)**
> Rock the Vote is dedicated to protecting freedom of expression and empowering young people to change the world. RTV Community Street Teams take civic engagement to the streets by registering people to vote and distributing information at concerts and other events.
> www.rockthevote.org

to protecting the Internet for teens, to using "guerilla" tactics such as teaching people how to disable Internet blocking software. They even work internationally, showing people how to disable the blocking software that China uses on all computers in their country. Our generation is far too savvy to be blocked by software and far too outspoken to let such egregious threats to free speech go unchallenged.[39]

Technology affects not only political issues, but also the political process. Campaigns fundraise, organize, and sell their messages online. Email updates are becoming more advanced and provide a free forum for candidates to reach their constituents. Governor Jesse Ventura's (I-MN) well-organized campaign was empowered by email alerts and online

---

[39] See peacefire.org.

fundraising. In the four days after the New Hampshire Primary, Senator John McCain (R-AZ) "netted $2 million on the Internet."[40] Presidential candidate and Governor Howard Dean (D-VT) used meetup.com to organize thousands of volunteers across the country. Issue advocacy groups increasingly are utilizing the web to educate the public, lobby Congress, and build coalitions. In 1998, one in five young people went online first for reliable information on candidates and elections.[41] According to another survey in 2001, "21 percent of 18-24 year-olds logged on to learn about party policies, compared to 8 percent of 25-44 year-olds."[42] By 2002, about eighty percent of all people (not just Millennials) went online to get information on where candidates stood on issues.[43] The how and where of the political process has changed completely in one decade.

The Media and Politics

Technology is not the only factor that shapes our socialization. The media, commonly referred to as the fourth estate, plays a major role in politics today. When the framers of our constitution established the balance of powers through the Executive, Legislative, and Judicial branches of government, they thought that would be enough. But time marches forward and ever since Deep Throat uncovered Tricky Dick in the 1970s, the media set up a full-time business in Washington and never left the city.

While any Joe, Jane, Jamal, Juanita, or Ji Millennial with access to a computer can join a discussion group, get a newsletter, or become self-educated about issues that inspire them, alternative media neither educates nor shapes the

---

[40] Mallaby, Sebastian. "McCain's E-Politics." *WashPost*, 03/04/00 p. A17.
[41] National Association of Secretaries of State, New Millennium Study 1998. stateofthevote.org (a.k.a. *NASSMillennium*)
[42] NetPulse Vol. 5 No. 15. *PoliticsOnline.com*, 08/01/01
[43] Pew Internet Project, Press Release 1/5/03--The Internet and Campaign 2002 pewinternet.org/releases/release.asp?id=58

collective unconscious of society. Tom Brokaw reaches millions more people in a couple of weeks than Matt Drudge ever will in his lifetime. *Salon* magazine cannot hold a candle to the size of *Newsweek*'s readership. Alternet.org and the Independent Media Center are not a balance to Fox News. Channel One[44] reaches more kids than all the other networks combined, but it is just a different corporate format, not "alternative."

Popular mainstream media has its benefits. It helps unify and educate a diverse and piebald country by creating a common American experience. However, when the media is so consolidated that healthy debate of political issues ceases to exist, our country is robbed of the type of fresh ideas, and diverse points of view like those that founded our nation. In response, media experts and activists gathered in 2002 at Musgrove – an important political conference center in Georgia. After a solid weekend of presentations and discussions, this group formed the Declaration of Digital Democracy (DDD). These activists were concerned that most of the country's major newspapers, radio stations, television networks, and cable systems should not be owned by a dozen conglomerates, all not coincidently run by white males. They wanted to ensure that the Internet would remain an open marketplace of ideas and this coalition continues to fight the consolidation of the media.

As a generation of rising activists, we need to be more aware of the media issue. As Colorado activist Nell Geiser says, "Unless young people seriously rise up and take control of the media, we're screwed."[45] We don't want our media to have a liberal, conservative or corporate bias. The openness of the media will shape what independent political thinkers can say, and could even stifle creativity in the music industry. Can you imagine a world where you could only listen to polka, cumbia, or

---

[44] "The Channel One Network is a learning community of 12,000 American middle, junior and high schools representing over 8 million students and 400,000 educators." See: ChannelOne.com. Viewed on 7/1/03
[45] *Future500*, p. 21.

doowop? Every station playing the same mixed up beat with hits from Poland?! This is what could happen to our political voice and our musical selections.

Before the FCC made a decision in the spring of 2003 to allow further consolidation of TV and radio stations, 400 protesters packed an FCC meeting to challenge the change. Dozens of speakers at the hearing warned, "that mergers resulting from looser rules could leave a few huge corporations in control of what people watch, hear, and read. That in turn, many stated, would threaten the vigor of democracy, which relies upon a system of public debate representing a range of viewpoints."[46] In addition to this protest, 500,000 people sent in emails and post cards opposing the consolidation. Although these protests were not all youth led (both the National Rifle Association and the National Organization for Women opposed the new rule) many Millennials stood up to protest this decision.

The effect of these new rules on the Internet may be the most dangerous and offensive threat to our generation. Internet outlets that do reach millions of people, namely AOL, merged with the traditional media. The formerly independent media that kept a close eye on society and raised a critical voice to Washington now has a huge vested interest in the status quo. And now, regardless of how liberal or conservative our political outlets may be – they still refuse to acknowledge the power of Millennials. If it's not about us destroying, killing or maiming each other, then there's no room on the six o'clock evening news to report it.

Have you heard the story about the kids in Baltimore who started their own coffee house to give back to the community? Did you see it on TV, hear about it on the radio, or read it in the newspaper? No! No surprise there. It was, however, on the Internet. The growth of independent media has been made

---

[46] "Huge turnout at FCC meeting" *The Argus*, 4/29/03.
theargusonline.com/Stories/0,1413,83~1971~1357420,00.html

possible by the Internet and fueled by interest from our generation. Freedom of speech is alive and well online – it does not as easily succumb to partisanship or political correctness. The future of this digital freedom is critical to our generation. We need more media outlets like "What Kids Can Do,"[47] and less media moguls perpetuating the myth that kids can't do anything.

Case Study: Alternative Media Library
Michelle Chen started the Alternative Media Library and Resource Center (AMLRC) in New Haven, Connecticut as a way to empower alternative artists to harness the power of the media for social change. The AMLRC is a media collection of magazines, digital video, underground music, amateur movies, art and more from around the country. The Center facilitates activist workshops, organizes open mic nights, and hosts film festivals. The AMLRC has created a safe space for artists to share ideas and resources and effect social change.

Youth Activist Step #2
Educate Yourself
Michelle searched for places to learn about alternative media and found none. The AMLRC is a place for people to educate themselves about the art and activism of alternative media.

How Media Shapes Politics

If the media shapes the way we think and what we think about, then what does that mean for Millennial Politics? Politically, the rise of the power of the media over the past four decades has come at the expense of other institutions, including political parties. Primaries have replaced party caucuses and candidates experiences and stance on issues is increasingly more important than their political affiliation in determining how

---

[47] What Kids Can Do is a website dedicated to telling positive stories about young people. See: whatkidscando.org.

people (specifically those critical swing voters) vote.[48] The media has chosen to focus on personal stories and "the horse race"[49] rather than the issues. This coverage turns many people off to politics and does little to further the political debate about critical, unresolved, social issues.

In addition, the expense of the commercial media forces candidates to spend more time fundraising than actually campaigning, so money becomes more important than issues (and often dictates who wins). The elite (those same guys who own the papers and are in control) have more access to politicians than regular people because of the way the system is now set up. And the elite are not about to change that.

Despite some changes in campaign finance law, the media remains the biggest culprit in our hyper-expensive system of elections. According to legendary CBS anchorman Walter Cronkite, "Candidates should not have to put themselves on the auction block to raise the resources needed to communicate in the modern era."[50] However, there is a solution to this problem. Since the airwaves are owned by the public and lent to 1,300 broadcast stations in the United States for free, these stations have a legal obligation to act in the public interest. However, they are profiting off of our broken political system by fleecing candidates with the price of campaign commercials and short changing the public with very little issue based coverage. But, we won't accept the belief that this is just the American way.

Music, Art and Politics

Rock the Vote (RTV) was created in 1990 in response to the government labeling

---

[48] "Key Findings on Opportunities for Candidates: What are Youth Looking For?" Center for Democracy and Citizenship. See: youngcitizensurvey.org/candidates.htm.

[49] News stories about the 'horse race' would focus on who is winning and by how much and have nothing to do with the issues of the campaign, or even the reasons for why they are winning.

[50] Taylor, Paul. "The Case for Free Air Time." *ABCampaigns*, 03/00, p. 2.

which music albums were inappropriate for youth. Rock the Vote's goal was to reverse the trend of decreased voting among eighteen- to thirty-five-year-olds. With help from the music industry, RTV tried to make voting cool with public service announcements of Madonna wearing nothing but an American flag encouraging kids to register and vote. RTV organized concerts, registered people to vote and even showed up on the West Wing encouraging young people to get involved. Most significantly, they convinced the Democrat Presidential candidates in 2003 to have a youth debate on CNN viewed by three million people.

Rock the Vote isn't the only group using music to encourage voting. Their sister organization Rap the Vote is at countless events registering people and 2003 saw the launch of a new group called Punkvoter.com to mobilize the punk scene. Jello Biafra, a punk icon active with Punkvoter announced, "I'm here because voting matters. I'm all for insurrection in the street, but it doesn't' accomplish much without insurrection at the ballot box."[51]

Music isn't used only to encourage voting. Much like previous social movements, art and music have been used at political rallies and to give life to the activist's voice. Fifteen-foot-large paper maché puppets protest the WTO and youth create posters to promote the end gun violence. Guerrilla Theater advocates for worker's rights and activists play KRS-One's music and attend Beastie Boys' concerts to "Free Tibet." The Dixie Chicks question the war; American Idol candidates salute the flag; and, Christian Rock inspires segments of our generation. The proliferation of MP3s allows us to hear music – and whatever political message may be associated with it – all for free.

---

[51] Dufour, Jeff. "Punkvoter tries to spur youth turnout." *The Hill*, 11/5/03. See: www.thehill.com/living/110503_punkvoter.aspx.

Some organizations, like the Underground Railroad out of San Francisco, are weaving art and politics together in a tapestry of paintbrushes and picket signs and an orchestra of microphones and megaphones. In 1997, five Bay Area youth of color from the Universal Zulu Nation came together, "integrating art, culture, spirituality, and revolutionary politics in cultural events using dance, song, spoken word, hip hop, and visual art,"[52] to convey their messages. The group has grown significantly in the last few years and clearly demonstrates how many young artists use their skills and talents to encourage activism and not just provide entertainment.

Television, Movies, Radio and Politics

We may be young but we are already making a name for ourselves in political media. Chaille Stoval followed the 2000 election from the New Hampshire Primaries to the Florida controversy. With his digital video camera he filmed a full-length documentary called *Party Animals* on the race and interviewed every candidate along the way. This ten-year-old reporter was able to use the media to make sure that our generation was heard.

The media was different for Gen Xers – our older siblings and cousins grew up with the *World Wrestling Federation (WWF)* on TV and *Slacker* on the big screen. Meanwhile, *The West Wing* and *Spy Kids* are socializing our generation. Politics is becoming part of popular culture. Candidates go on *Oprah*; and, *People Magazine* follows former Presidents. Even the *WWF* (now the *WWE or World Wrestling Entertainment*) has gotten into the act as wrestling superstars encourage young people to vote and get involved.[53] At night, Jay Leno gives us a unique view of world events and Jon Stewart delivers comedy

---

[52] See: underground-railroad.org/herstory.html. Viewed on 6/1/03.
[53] About 400,000 new voters were registered through the WWE Smack Down Your Vote from 1999-2003. youthvote.org/members/partners/wwe.htm

and world events on the *Daily Show*. Youth Radio combines music, poetry and politics. However, don't misread this trend: this is not the simplification of politics, but the re-democratization. Our generation is savvy – we know the difference between substance and style and we are tired of sound bites that say little and accomplish less.

In fact, the traditional political establishment could learn a thing or two from the popular media. Democratic Governor and Presidential candidate Howard Dean of Vermont seems to be emulating fictional President Bartlett from *The West Wing* with his straight-talking, liberal, intellectualism. Our election commission should consider watching *American Idol* – about twice as many Millennials ages 18-25 voted to choose our *American Idol* in 2002 than voted for our American President in 2000.[54] Millennials are willing to vote, but let us text our message and be sure whoever gets the most votes actually wins (neither Bush *nor* Clinton had a majority when they first took office).

Millennial Paul Revere

As a generation we are not yet fully engaged and we need to be. Technology and the media give us the tools to motivate and inspire. We need more youth-friendly programming like PBS's *Listen Up!* that focuses on youth leadership.[55] We need more youth-run cable shows that promote community activism like *Hard Cover* in Chicago. We need more youth-run television stations that give youth a voice like *TeenLineTV* in D.C. We need more sites like WireTap that feature, "youth in the pursuit of the dirty truth." We need to stop allowing others to define us as dumb, apathetic and dangerous; it is time for us to define our selves.

---

[54] Approximately 18 million people 18-25 voted for the American Idol finals and about 9 million people 18-25 voted in the Presidential Election.
[55] See millennialpolitics.com/links for information on *Listen Up!* and all of the other media outlets.

PART TWO:

THE ISSUES

"Brimming with idealism, far outstripping what we saw only a decade ago. Instead of knocking young men and women, we ought to be providing them with more opportunities to give back. The day is not far off when a year or more of service to the country will once again be enshrined as an essential part of becoming an American citizen." –
David Gergen[56]

3

AMERICA'S NEW CORPS

Volunteerism has been on a two-decade rise since the early 1980s when individual Gen Xers rejected traditional political or institutional forums for service and began volunteering as a method for social change. Since 1989, the percentage of incoming freshman who say they volunteered in high school has increased fifteen percent (from 66% to 81%).[57] In the 1960s and 70s, "volunteering" or "service" typically referred to going into the military or cleaning out latrines because you were a conscientious objector. Now with service learning, high school service requirements, and the creation of AmeriCorps and the Freedom Corps,[58] volunteerism has taken off among Millennials. Furthermore, volunteerism no longer merely means, "giving back to the community" – it has increasingly become a forum with which to change and shape society in positive ways. Service, whether in the context of the military, the community,

---

[56] Gergen, David. "A Time to Heed the Call." 12/24/01 *USNews*, p. 60.
[57] *HERI/UCLA*, 1984 to 2000.
[58] The government's role in national service goes back as late at the Great Depression. More recently President Clinton created AmeriCorps in 1992 as a "domestic peace corps." AmeriCorps grew and by 2002 President Bush changed it a little and called it the "Freedom Corps." City Year, another large-scale service program, is generally under the same "Freedom Corps" umbrella.

or the school, has political implications as one of the most important issues for our generation.

Many naysayers dismiss the spike in volunteerism as a result of increased high school requirements, pressure to get into college and service learning programs. However, whatever the cause, volunteerism isn't just omnipresent, it is also en vogue. Despite the strong economy's pull to paid employment during the late 1990s, the Peace Corps grew in size every year, as did the newly created AmeriCorps program. In fact, Millennials embraced AmeriCorps much more quickly than Boomers rushed into the Peace Corps at its inception. By October 1998 "the four-year-old AmeriCorps program [had] inducted its 100,000th volunteer. The Peace Corps took twenty years to reach the same milestone."[59] By the seventh year of the program the numbers increased to 200,000 people which took the Peace Corps forty years to reach.[60] Eighty-one percent of our generation supports expanding AmeriCorps to give every young person the opportunity to participate in a full year of national community service. Despite the success of this program, Congress' commitment has wavered from year to year and funding for this social program always seems shaky.

While these government-funded service programs explicitly prohibit volunteers from engaging in political behavior (an institutional quirk which disproportionately discourages younger people from participating in politics – even when not on the job), alumni of these programs became more politically active citizens as a result of their service.[61]

In 1990, Strauss and Howe identified Millennials as a civic generation in their book *Generations*. Like our G.I. grandparents or great-grandparents, Millennials are very socially conscious. "The Millennium Project found that youth volunteering is

---

[59] Clinton, President William. "Remarks to AmeriCorps Volunteers." 01/18/99

[60] Clinton, President William. "Remarks at the Martin Luther King Jr. Day Celebration." 01/15/01

[61] According to 1994 City Year Alumni Survey. See cityyear.org/alumni/lacy.cfm.

increasing and is at record high numbers: while in 1989, 55 percent of 15 to 24-year-olds said they helped an elderly neighbor in the past, ten years later 87 percent reported having done this same volunteer activity."[62] The call to service is so strong among American youth that our generation will rise to any challenges that the older generation bring to the table, such as Senator John Kerry's proposal to make service a requirement for high school graduation. In fact, many Millennials subscribe to the philosophy of the bolder the better. If Congress were to institute a national program of service that required all youth between the ages of 18-25 to commit nine months of service to this country, either in the military, the Freedom Corps or the Peace Corps, our generation would answer the call.[63]

A year of national service would, "forge bonds of community at a time when technology is pushing all aspects of society toward individual customization, [and] instill a sense of public spirit and community obligation in the [generation]."[64] As Zach Clayton, the seventeen-year-old President of the National Association of Student Councils said in his high school commencement speech, "If we all spent a year of our life in the Peace Corp, in Freedom Corp, Teach for America, or the military, we would breathe new life into democracy and freedom, we would be bound together by a common service, and on the 4th of July, we might just think a little harder about what our forefathers have sacrificed."[65] Not every teenager would be jumping up and down excited about the prospect, but you would not find college students burning the 21st century "draft" cards or starting an exodus to Canada.

---

[62] *NASSMillennium*
[63] "66% of 15-25 year olds would support a draft that gives people the choice between civilian and military service." According to: Trust Matters, "Is Anyone Listening." An Issue Report from the Partnership for Trust in Government. N. 1, Spring 2002, p. 38. See: youngcitizensurvey.org. (a.k.a *TrustMatters*)
[64] Cherny, Andrei. The Next Deal, p. 237.
[65] Clayton, Zach. High School Valedictory Address, 05/31/03.

Community service perfectly exemplifies an act that should now be considered political action, although it has traditionally fallen under the umbrella of non-political pursuits. As E.J. Dionne writes, "The greatest reforming generations are the ones that marry the aspirations of service to the possibilities of politics and harness the good work done in local communities to transform a nation."[66] Twenty-six-year-old City Year alum Jim Balfanz says it best: "I used to see politics as a two-party system, with one ideology against the other. Now I see it as engaging citizens in trying to solve problems."[67]

We are doing this today. When students decide to take Spring Break in Appalachia volunteering rather than drinking in the Real Cancun, they raise their political voices. Likewise, we express our politics when we volunteer with AIDS organizations and tutor children in under funded school districts. This type of action takes a different approach than writing letters to HUD to increase support for the homeless, protesting low funding levels for AIDS research, or rallying on Congress to protect education spending – but it qualifies as political action because it seeks to change society. In many ways, we believe this action is more effective than writing letters to Congress that generates responses with letters from Millennials interning on the Hill.

United Leaders

Increasingly our generation is uniting behind this concept of renewing public service. Two graduates from Tufts University understood the pulse of  the generation and founded an organization . called "United Leaders." Well before media experts declared 9-11 would galvanize our generation, Jesse Levey and Larry Harris of United

---

[66] *NewStudentPolitics*, p. 20.
[67] Huang, Thomas. "Common Ground; City Year service gives young people a citizenship lesson." *The Dallas Morning News*, 05/19/06. p. 1F.

Leaders created a summer institute for public service based out of Harvard University. By focusing on the "service gap," United Leaders seeks to connect volunteer work with political and social change. United Leaders has tapped into an important theme for young activists that was articulated in the 2000 National Youth Platform: "While we support and encourage community service, it is crucial that service does not replace one's participation in our democracy."[68]

Years before our generational power began to grow, United Leaders began creating the institutions to coordinate young elected officials and motivate our generational peers to action. The "City Year"[69] of politics, United Leaders will motivate our generation to public service as City Year motivated Xers and now Millennials to community service.

Case Study: Jr. ManaTEENS.

Laura Lockwood founded the ManaTEEN Club in 1994 to promote youth volunteerism. Laura and her team coordinate supervised Saturday morning volunteer projects for young people, including painting homes for underprivileged families, assessing the safety needs of senior citizens, and planting and maintaining local gardens.

"Engaging children as volunteers helps bridge the gap in our community," she explains. "Kids are seen as responsible, caring, and compassionate residents, not just 'the noisy kids down the street.'"

Youth Activism Step #3
Start (or Join) a Group

When Laura first tried to do volunteer work she was not given substantial opportunities to make a difference because of her age. So she started her own group and empowered over 10,000 people to take action.

---

[68] 2000 National Youth Platform. Foundation of America: Youth in Action, p. 2. (a.k.a. *NYP 2000*)

[69] City Year is "An Action Tank for national service. City Year seeks to demonstrate, improve and promote the concept of national service as a means for building a stronger democracy." See cityyear.org.

Environmentalism

Youth service pays particular attention to the issue of the environment. The modern environmental movement celebrates three decades of activism; for the first time in history, Millennials on the left and the right have grown up accepting the belief that our environment is not only in danger, but also influenced heavily by our actions. We were all teenagers or younger on the 25th Anniversary of Earth Day. The debate on such issues as global warming has shifted from, "Does this exist?" to "What, if anything, should we do about it?" The stereotype that our generation is pro-environment rings true in the statistic that in 2000, two-thirds of 16-25 year-olds "felt there should be stronger environmental leadership, laws and penalties for violations of these laws."[70] However, like so many other hot political issues of the day, Millennials are striving for practical, middle of the road solutions that reject the radicalism of fanatical liberals and the dangerous disregard of extreme conservatives.

From large environmental organizations like the Center for Environmental Citizenship and the Student Environmental Action Coalition to smaller, community, youth-run groups like Arlingtonians for Recycling (in VA) and Caring for a Coastal Environment (in CA), Millennials are actively advocating for a cleaner environment in high schools and colleges.

Some of our generation's few spokespeople and young role models have been environmental leaders. Adam Werbach, the youngest-ever Sierra Club President, showed our generation that we did not need to wait to make a major difference. Similarly, at age nine, Millennial Melissa Poe started an international non-profit called KIDS F.A.C.E[71] to save the environment after

---

[70] Raducha, Peter. "Preliminary Results of a Nationwide Survey of Youth." Oregon State University: The Program for Governmental Research and Education, 07/00 (a.k.a. *NatYouthSurvey2000*)

[71] KIDS F.A.C.E stands for Kids For A Clean Environment. For more information see: kidsface.org.

seeing an episode of "Highway to Heaven" about what the world might look like in fifty years. Millennial author and activist Danny Seo founded Earth 2000 at age thirteen. Danny became a regular spokesperson for environmental living, the People magazine poster child for a generation that did not perceive vegetarians as freaks, animal rights as weird, or recycling as the be all and end all of environmentalism. In fact, according to a national study by Teenage Research Unlimited in Northbrook, Illinois, nearly a quarter of teens consider being a vegetarian to be "cool." Furthermore, fifteen percent of college students are some type of vegetarian;[72] this diet is no longer relegated to "granola" teens who don't shower. Our diets may change and our commitment to recycling may even waiver, but this generation is making a life long dedication to protecting the environment.

Youth Social Entrepreneurship

The social entrepreneurship demonstrated by Melissa and Danny is a hallmark of this generation and needs backing to grow and flourish. For this purpose, organizations like Youth Venture support young leaders who are creating their own civic-minded organizations, clubs, or businesses that give back to the community. Youth Venture's founder Bill Drayton believes youth social entrepreneurship is about more than supporting kids who want to make a difference; it is "a transformative youth movement which is changing the way society looks at young people."[73] He's right, and our generation is embracing the opportunity. We are beginning to change the perception of youths' years from "can't do incompetence" to "can do initiative."

---

[72] National Restaurant Survey. Some polls (PETA) have that percentage as high as 20%.
[73] See youthventure.org.

Youth Philanthropy

Organizations like Youth Venture and the Active Element Foundation (AEF) connect traditional philanthropy with youth activism. Three accomplished young activists, Billy Wimsatt, Kofi Taha, and Gita Drury launched the AEF to support other young activists. AEF supports not only the most pressing issues facing young people, but also the most innovative youth-run organizations fighting for social change. These types of organizations are multiplying. A number of other groups were either started or grew significantly in the late 1990s including: Do Something, Youth As Resources, Reach Your Peak, Start Something, ShiNE, I Do Foundation, and the 2100 Fund – each with their own approach to youth philanthropy.[74]

Service Vote 2000

Youth Service America tried to bridge service and politics in 2000 by launching Service Vote 2000. Service Vote launched a campaign to teach people that politics and service are two sides of the same coin of civic engagement. One successful PSA showed kids cleaning up a beach in the summers of '98 and '99. The next scene read, "What are you going to do this November on Election Day to make sure you don't have to clean up the beach again next year?" The commercials were very compelling but not widely seen.

> **Youth Activism Resource:**
> **Youth Service America**
> YSA is a resource center and premier alliance of 300+ organizations committed to increasing the quantity and quality of opportunities for young Americans to serve locally, nationally, or globally. They have a wonderful email list about youth service and are an incredible clearinghouse of youth volunteer organizations.
> www.ysa.org

---

[74] See MillennialPolitics.com for more information about these organizations.

The 2000 presidential candidates themselves represented a wide range of environmental beliefs. Bush believed in free market environmentalism and Gore had a record of modest environmental progress and a best-selling book on the issue. Nader was a strong environmentalist who attacked the missed opportunities of Democrats and laissez-faire attitude of Republicans. After Bush was elected, environmental issues became even more important to many of us. Anxiety over arsenic in the water, energy policy, global warming, biotech, and the oil crises were of great concern to our generation. Concerns over the environment were all over the media[75] until 9-11 gave us more immediate issues to worry about.

Millennial Solutions

We as a generation are often mischaracterized as a liberal block when it comes to the environment and community service. However, this misses the big picture. Many Millennials approach these issues with business principles in mind. Good business includes encouraging service to our country. Effective volunteerism uses the principles of social entrepreneurship. More public service can translate into smaller government. Instead of a new federal department to solve our problems, we need citizens willing to roll up their sleeves to make a difference. Helping the environment can also be good for the country. In Texas the wind power business is expected to grow 1,000 percent over the next decade, bringing the state billions of dollars.[76] There is literally a windfall to be made in America and overseas on efficient, clean technologies. Mother Earth and Wall Street are not mutually exclusive choices and we should stop treating them that way.

---

[75] Schneider, Keith. "The Right Stuff" *Grist Magazine*, 08/30/01.
gristmagazine.com/maindish/schneider083001.asp
[76] "Report: 'Clean energy' market to charge to $89B" *Austin Business Journal*, 2/20/03
austin.bizjournals.com/austin/stories/2003/02/17/daily32.html

"The demographic trends are unmistakable. Projections indicate that over the next twenty years, women and people of color will constitute a growing majority of new entrants into the American labor market. The Millennium Generation, today's 15-to-25-year-olds, is the most racially mixed generation in our history. Diversity is already an imperative for the business community. Corporate America was among the first to recognize that diversity pays dividends. CEOs know that organizations which value diversity - and know how to use it - will have the competitive edge, not only in recruiting and retaining the best employees, but in operating successfully worldwide."
— *George Tenet, Director of the CIA*

4

HIP HOP HUMAN RIGHTS

Gone are days of black and white televisions, and so too are the days when civil rights were a bipolar conflict. Our generation uses the term "human rights" rather than civil rights, because the phrase more fully embodies all of the issues of discrimination with which our society still struggles. Human rights include ending discrimination based on: age, sexual orientation, gender identity, physical disability, multiracial status, religious beliefs, national origin, or immigrant status. Human rights still means that it is not okay to pull over a black man because he is driving an expensive car or pay a woman seventy-six cents to the working *man's* dollar.[77] We want to end all of the "isms" and the "phobias." Human rights are an important issue for this generation, but one that is increasingly being solved by demographics, individual initiative, and a changing society. For these reasons we are less likely than Boomers or Xers to fight for civil rights or gender equality –

---

[77] Soares, Claire. "Study: Women Earn a Quarter Less Than Men." *Reuters*, 4/3/01.

why fight for a women's studies department at a school with 57% women; why fight for traditional affirmative action when money not race influences educational opportunity. Over ten percent of the total U.S. population is foreign born – 28.4 million people![78] Members of the Millennial Generation "are sixty percent more likely to be nonwhite than those of [our] parents' and grandparents' generations."[79] "As of 2002, nonwhites and Latinos accounted for 37 percent of the 20-or-under population."[80] The cultural, racial, and ethnic diversity of the country is most visible in states like Florida, Texas, New York and California, but in a few short decades this diversity will be present everywhere. How Miami, New York City and San Diego handle becoming "majorityless cities" will be very telling of the future of America. In California and Texas in 1998 the most common baby name for a boy was Juan. No longer will Caucasian babies named Jack and Jill demand the majority of the states' resources and attention. (Although we definitely need to worry about Jack and Jill as they go over the hill to retire.)

In a 1998 interview with former Governor Gray Davis (D-CA) about the diversity of California, he said that he would not be surprised if he were the last white male to be Governor of California.[81] He, of course, could never have predicted that Governor Arnold Schwarzenegger would get the spot from him. Arnold may be white but he is an immigrant. This is a significant fact in California (albeit much less important than his star status), a state so diverse that it is the first to have no racial majority population. Demographers thought this switch would happen in the early 21st century, but in fact, it happened in the mid-1990s.

---

[78] *Census.*
[79] Chideya, Farai. "Shades of the Future; Will race provide the mid-century crisis?" *Time*, 02/01/99, p. 54.
[80] *Millennials2College*, p. 23.
[81] Conversation with Scott Beale at NGA New Governors' Meeting 12/98.

Affirmative Action

In 1994, California responded to the growing minority population by passing Proposition 187, cutting off some health and social services – including access to public education – to illegal aliens and their children. That initiative was put on hold by a federal court, but the vote helped set the stage for a national debate on immigration. The passage of Proposition 187, among other things, triggered a series of events that led California, Texas, and Florida to eliminate affirmative action for admissions to public universities. When the debate over this issue took the State of Michigan to the U.S. Supreme Court in 2003, the White House argued diversity is a compelling "good" on college campuses, but that there were race neutral ways to reach that goal (like taking into account hardship or accepting the top ten percent of all high school students). "Fifty-four percent of college students support affirmative action programs for minorities and women for admission to colleges and universities."[82] This is not very strong support for an old program. In fact, according to the UCLA survey of college freshman agree "strongly" or "somewhat" that, "affirmative action in college admission should be abolished."[83] But before we

> **Youth Activism Resource: Listen, Inc.**
>
> Listen, Inc. recruits urban youth with a social justice mission and supports these Millennial activists with trainings workshops, networking opportunities, mentors, research and more to assist their civic engagement projects.
> www.lisn.org

go any further, this issue so quickly gets wrapped into socio economic class in modern society that we've decided to take an even closer look at affirmative action in Chapter Eight.

---

[82] *CampusKids*, p. 6.
[83] *Millennials2College*, p. 60.

Politics of Race

"Youth-race politics" is not the same as "traditional race politics" for a number of reasons. These reasons include the size of racial minorities in our generation, the number of multi-racial Millennials, the degree of racial integration, and our level of race and party identification. Simply put, times have changed. "It may be little appreciated, but 40 years ago expressions of overt racism were regular and easily made by many persons, including leaders in the United States. By the 1990s, those expressing overtly racist views were not well received; it is presently socially undesirable to hold such views, and it is unacceptable, except among small isolated and marginal groups, for anyone to express overtly racist attitudes."[84] Boomers lived in a different world, where, even in the 1980s KKK leaders like David Duke were able to win public office.[85]

Due to this evolution in society, African American Millennials do not behave in similar political ways as older African Americans. According to the Joint Center for Political and Economic Studies, young Blacks do not identify as strongly with Democrats as their parents and grand parents and do not see the Republican Party as a viable alternative. In today's hyper-partisan times, this leaves young Blacks without a unified political voice.

Simultaneously, growing Latino populations all over the country began to demand attention. The Hispanic voter became a hot commodity in the 2000 Election when both parties tried to capitalize on the rising tide of Latino populations in the United States. President Bush reached out to the Latino voter by speaking Spanish at events and airing TV commercials in Spanish. While generally supportive of President Bush, Latinos

---

[84] Bositis, David. "Diverging Generations" Washington, DC: Joint Center for Political and Economic Studies, 2000, p. 23. (a.k.a *DivGen*)

[85] David Duke won a seat representing Metairie, Louisiana, in the Louisiana State Legislature in 1989. Five unsuccessful political campaigns followed, including a 1992 bid for the U.S. Presidency.

have not yet moved en masse to the Republican Party, leaving this important voting bloc is up for grabs. Quite frankly, it remains to be seen if this diverse ethnic group will always vote in a bloc. Or, for that matter, whether they will become a voting force at all since young Latino voter registration and turnout rates fall far behind those of both Black and White youth.[86]

In 2002 the Texas Democratic Party proclaimed a "dream ticket" with a Latino for Governor and an African American for Senate. However, since this dream ticket came up short, it puts into question the value of race-based politics (or the ability of any Democrat to win state-wide in Texas).

Case Study: Students United for Racial Equity.
In February 2002, Palo Alto based twenty-year-old Nina Sung created Students United for Racial Equity (SURE). Growing up as one of the only minority students in her high school, Nina became motivated to create race dialogue sessions after she participated in one herself. Nina explains, "My goal is to provide a forum for local high school juniors and seniors to explore the significance of race as it is reflected in psychological, social, and economic well-being."

Nina created a fourteen-session seminar to discuss pre-assigned readings and assignments. "SURE is designed to give young people an opportunity to discuss the meaning of race as it presents itself in today's society; through academic readings and individual research projects, student will explore a more inclusive curriculum," She explains. Though launching modestly and strategically, Nina's ultimate goal is to leverage her initial dialogue sessions as a model for replication in schools nationwide.

Youth Activist Step #4
Find Your Vision
Nina's vision was a race blind society. Before taking any other steps she articulated her mission by naming her organization – it would become "Students United for Racial Equality."

Race is a complicated issue in our country and it is too often simplified, misunderstood

---

[86] Lopez, Mark Hugo. "Civic Engagement Among Minority Youth." *CIRCLE.*

or ignored in politics. While rarely the sole factor in deciding how one will vote, race does significantly impact many voting decisions. Groups like Black Youth Vote and the National Council of La Raza are effective organizers and motivators, and research supports the notion that race is a big motivator in turnout.[87]

Hip Hop Activism

One method to motivate youth, especially minority youth in our generation is manifested in the Hip Hop movement. The public perceives most organized youth activism as very white, wealthy and suburban. Hip Hop shatters that stereotype. A number of Hip Hop activists have created The League of Young Voters to educate young people about political and social issues and current candidates. Rap the Vote, Listen, Inc., Beats for Peace, Democracy Summer, and Hip Hop Summits at Harvard try to connect urban teens with beltway politics. As Chuck D told author Scott Beale in an interview in 1996, "I could care less who people vote for, but people got to vote, especially young blacks who are getting ignored by the system."

Hip Hop's involvement with youth activism not only brings more color to the protests, but also makes it a lot cooler to be active. As the recently published Future 500 directory of youth activism groups notes, "right now it is almost becoming cool for young people to be political. We've got major recording artists going to Cuba for Mumia benefit shows and Russell Simmons and Def Jam's roster mobilizing tens of thousands of high school students in NYC to protest education cuts."[88]

---

[87] According to *DivGen*, p.24, "By a large margin (64.9% to 30.6%), the youngest blacks believed that black voters would vote for a black candidate over the most qualified candidate regardless of race. The oldest blacks, by an even larger margin, believed the opposite."
[88] *Future500*, p. 3.

Gay and Lesbian Rights

Human rights are as much about sexual orientation as they are about race. It is simply not acceptable to discriminate against people on the basis of sexual orientation. GLBTTQ (Gay, Lesbian, Bisexual, Transgender, Transsexual, and Questioning) is a well-known acronym for our generation. According to Benjie Nycum, "There are more than 2,000 gay-straight alliances in schools in the U.S., and they're popping up all over."[89] Even among religious and conservative Millennials, our generation feels that one's sexual orientation is their own business. "Attitudes about homosexuality, for instance, have seen a dramatic shift since the late 1980s. Then, about 50 percent [of youth] said laws were needed to prohibit homosexual relations. The number dropped to 25 percent in 2002."[90] According to the Kaiser Family Foundation, 61 percent of Millennials "favor providing legal rights to gays and lesbians for civil unions."[91] [92]

Clearly, though, homophobia still exists. In a 1999 national school survey of gay students conducted by the Gay, Lesbian and Straight Education Network, 91 percent said they regularly heard homophobic remarks at school, and nearly 40 percent of the time the comments came from school faculty or staff members. But for homosexual Millennials, life is certainly better than it was ten years ago. Seattle, Cleveland, New Orleans and New York are among many cities that have "gay" proms at the end of the school year – this is not your father's prom.

---

[89] Lotozo, Eils. "Pair Document the Gay Youths." *Philadelphia Inquirer*, 06/03/03, Lifestyle Section.

[90] Bluey, Robert B. "Youth Attitudes on Abortion Encourage Pro-Life Groups." CNSNews Service, 04/06/03.

[91] Kaiser Family Foundation. Press Release. "New Survey Shows Most Young Adults have Strong Opinions on Top Campaign Issues, But Many Still Not Planning to Vote." 09/25/00. See: kff.org/content/2000/3058/PressRelease.PDF (a.k.a *KFFSurvey*)

[92] The logo in this paragraph is from the Human Rights Campaign. See: hrc.org.

The government should neither bestow special rights nor restrictions on those with different lifestyles. Further, politicians who say they have no problem with homosexuals but a problem with homosexual acts should remember that Millennials on the left and right want the government out of this issue.

Hate Crimes

Anyone who thinks that discrimination is just a 20th century problem that went the way of the rotary phone just needs to ask Robin Chen Delos how she spent her summer in 2002. Robin learned that the KKK was planning a march on Washington. You may suspect that this march would only include a few dozen retired Klansmen who had nothing better to do. However, it was much worse than that. Hundreds of white sheeted, sometimes young, always racist, xenophobes were going to show up in force. The Klan's numbers had grown since September 11th and they wanted to show the world. In response to this march, hundreds of young African Americans, some of them admittedly militant, also came to the rally. In response to the Black Power counter protest, several hundred police came to keep the peace.

Seventeen-year-old Robin showed up on the day of the march with dozens of other young people holding up a banner that said "SHINE – Stop Hate, Inspire Neighborly Engagement." The group played drums, passed out fliers and tried to be a calm voice in what was a bizarre scene of police mounted on horses, young Black leaders shouting in bull horns and a big metal fence protecting the Klan on the front lawn of the Capitol.

Nearly 10,000 hate crimes a year signify a big problem for our generation, and frankly, a problem being committed by and against many people in this generation. "Fifty-five percent of hate crimes are on the basis of race, 17.9 percent are based on religion and 16.2 percent based on sexual orientation."[93] The

---

[93] *NYP 2000*, p 6.

name Matthew Sheppard[94] means something to most of us and after 9-11 we witnessed a new brand of hate crimes for Arab, Muslim and Sikh Americans. Religion and nationality didn't even matter, even South Asian and Latino Millennials with browner skin experienced post-9-11 discrimination. Most of us believe that hate crimes need to be recognized by society, legislated against in the government,[95] and stopped by people all over the country. All crime is wrong, and one murder is not worse than another; but we denounce hate crimes as the extreme manifestation of racism, homophobia, discrimination and ignorance.

Gender Politics

Millennial women will continue to make progress within this generation and society because of some fundamental changes that have occurred. New technology fosters more collaborative working environments and emerging entrepreneurs have rejected some of the traditional hierarchical competitive models. Business paradigm shifts will continue to increasingly favor women, despite the significant dominance of male CEOs at Fortune 500 companies. For students today, "feminism is less of a cause and more of a given."[96] Just look at your local high school – women are leading student councils, class papers, and volunteer clubs. Now, as the first generation born after Title IX grows up, even the best athletes in many schools are females as men struggle to maintain the pretense of gender superiority.

Millennial women far outnumber Millennial men on college campuses, even at schools that just decades before weren't coed.[97] Further, there is a growing gender gap in voting between

---

[94] Matthew Sheppard is the Millennial gay student in Wyoming who was brutally murdered and tied to a fence for being gay on 10/12/98. His death created a national outcry for hate crimes legislation.
[95] "77% favor expanding hate crimes legislation to protect gays." According to *KFFSurvey.*
[96] *Millennials2College*, p. 65.
[97] "58% of all college freshmen are women." According to *Millennials2College*, p. 58.

young men and women as more Millennial women regularly turn out to vote than men. Despite these trends, Congress remains a boys' club, there are far too few female Governors, and the judiciary has a lot of testosterone.

Our generation will change this. In fact, there is no question whether women or "minorities" will be leaders of this generation. The question that remains is – to what extent will white men play leadership roles? And, in a pluralistic society without one dominant voice, can one leader unite us all?

Youth Rights

Youth rights is an issue that has taken root in our generation and some young leaders have called it "the last civil rights movement." These young activists are struggling to end legal discrimination against young people. [98]

Today some kids are treated like servants performing chores for their families and/or pets showing off to their neighbors by singing holiday music. Legally and socially, youth under eighteen are not seen as full citizens and are treated as such. While most states prohibit discrimination against the

elderly, many places in this country give adults the right to discriminate against teenagers and youth. Like the women's movement and the civil rights movement of the previous century, youth rights activists are fighting laws that discriminate against

---

[98] Cartoon by Ben Livingston

young people such as the voting age, drinking age, curfews, anti-student laws and more. Like social movements before it, the youth rights movement hopes to change society's perceptions by changing laws that prevent youth from achieving their full potential.

The absurdity of some of these laws is sometimes laughable and sometimes tragic. Angela Lipsman, a fourteen-year-old girl in New York City, finished all of her high school requirements and was recruited to attend Vassar, but the state wouldn't grant her a high school equivalency diploma because she was not yet sixteen. Without the alternative high-school diploma, colleges wouldn't grant her a degree. In other words, myopic bureaucrats held this young woman back because of her age and the false notion that a gifted fourteen-year-old couldn't possibly be smart enough for a high school degree, even if she passed all the required tests.[99]

Society is constantly underestimating Millennials. Another example is thirteen-year-old Gregory Smith who graduated from Randolph Macon College in May 2003. By the time he graduated, he had already founded a group called International Peace Advocates and promoted peace on four different continents and the United Nations. This cum laude, mathematical brainchild hopes to one day be President and is a very tangible demonstration of what youth can achieve.[100]

The ageism that exists in our society is not just a shame, but it has tangible negative consequences. For example, in the media, youth violence is over-covered, while adult violence is often under-covered. "In 1997-1998, school murders occurred at about four a month. Parents murdering children at home clocked in at a half dozen per *day*."[101] The effect of this coverage is clear. A recent Gallup poll asked adults about youth crime rates.

---

[99] Campanile, Carl. "Girl Sues NY to be Grad at 14." *NYPost*, 04/21/03, p. 3.
[100] See: rmc.edu/directory/offices/mc/media/greg_smith_bio.asp Viewed on 06/01/03.
[101] Males, Mike. Framing Youth.

"The adults polled estimated that youth were responsible for 43 percent of violent crimes. The truth? FBI statistics show juveniles are responsible for thirteen percent of violent crimes, less than a third of what adults thought."[102] This, in turn, leads to parents demanding zero tolerance policies to address an overblown threat and ignores better solutions to the problems in our schools. [103]

We're beginning to speak out against these inequities and even more serious injustices overseas. Americans for a Society Free from Age Restrictions and the National Youth Rights Association (NYRA) are two organizations leading the charge in the United States for youth rights. NYRA has fought companies like Sharper Image, 7-11 and Blimpies that have signs on the their doors stating "Only Two Teenagers in the Store at One Time." We would not accept a store preventing the number of Blacks, Latinos or even senior citizens allowed inside, but discrimination against youth is somehow permissible. Our generation must remember that in our fight for human rights we must not forget the young.

Millennials are also having an impact overseas. Craig Kielburger founded an organization called Kids Can Free the Children (KCFTC) when he was twelve years old after he learned about young boys in Pakistan being sold into bondage. KCFTC has since become the largest international network of children helping children, with over 100,000 youth involved in 35 countries.

Race Matters

Cornell West was right; race does matter and we have a long way to go in achieving Martin Luther King's dream. We are staying true to the fight and each year youth-run groups like the

---

[102] Bervera, Sarah, Malkia Cyril and Ortega Yarborough. "When Perceptions Are Not Reality. Youth role in crime exaggerated." *SFChronicle*, 10/9/98, p. A25.
[103] For more info on Zero Tolerance, check out Chapter Nine.

Positive Youth Foundation in Greencastle, PA are moving the ball forward using music and culture to promote awareness of bigotry.[104] And now the flags of the civil war are finally coming off our state capitols, affirmative action is ready to be updated nationwide, and our definition of human rights is finally inclusive enough to include the blind kid, the gay guy, the Muslim girl, *and* the white pre-teen.

---

[104] See positive-youthfoundation.org.

"We have the university by the b#%&s, whatever way we twist them is going to hurt." – *Nati Passow, a University of Pennsylvania junior, in a meeting with his fellow anti-sweatshop protesters.*

5

SMALL WORLD

There are few youth issues that get more attention in the media than globalization; this fact alone is uniquely Millennial. Sixty years after Disney World added a ride for kids called Small World, the globe has become one large community. Our economic systems are closely tied to each other and we share cultural events with people all over the world. It took Christopher Columbus three months to cross the Atlantic in search of spices from India; it took less than a week for the "Spice Girls" to have their hit single "Tell Me What You Want" go number one on the pop charts in 125 countries.

Hundreds of thousands of Millennials have marched against globalization in Seattle, New York, DC, and places all over the country. Over 200 college campuses protested in unison against Nike and other international corporations for human rights violations. Two hundred and fifty high school and college campuses are part of the Student Global AIDS campaign. We are very aware of the world outside our national borders. But don't make a common mistake about us; we don't seek an end to internationalism, we seek to control globalization.

To many of us, globalization is the unchecked growth of international organizations and multinational corporations that make undemocratic decisions that affect local communities and developing nations. Internationalism is the economic interdependence and the exchange of cultures that enrich our lives and bring us all closer together.

Internationalism

In 1991, the first President Bush declared a New World Order. The Berlin Wall had fallen and a global coalition had formed to fight the first Gulf War. A few years later, President Clinton signed NAFTA (the North American Free Trade Agreement) opening the flow of trade in North America. Additionally, for two decades Europe has taken steps every year closer to a political and economic union. Formerly communist countries opened their doors to foreign trade and travelers; even the U.S. borders opened dramatically as annual immigration jumped 35 percent to over a million immigrants per year in the 1990s.[105] Even new controls on immigration after 9-11 cannot undo the change in America over the last decade. We have grown up in this diverse community and are hopeful that increased internationalism will decrease the likelihood of war (although perhaps not eliminate the need for it) and provide economic opportunities and political freedom for billions.

Despite our generation's internationalism, we're very proud to be Americans. Even before the flags became bestsellers in the fall of 2001, our generation wore American flags on t-shirts and U.S. Army fatigues to look cool. Within this nationalism, we, as Americans, feel we have an important role to play on the world stage. In fact, many of us want the country to be a more active international agent fighting against some of the rising forces we refer to as globalization. To be affective on the world stage we must not go alone; international organizations divide responsibility and multiply our chance for success. Many of us

---

[105] According to NumbersUSA.com.

are frustrated with bureaucratic hang-ups and the potential loss of sovereignty due to the United Nations, but our negative feelings and resentment for being let down by the Security Council during the 2003 war with Iraq are most targeted towards individual nations (France or the U.S. depending on where you stand) and not the entire institution.[106]

Case Study: United Students Against Sweatshops

In 1997, the UNITE summer interns began the Sweat-Free Campus Campaign. These interns joined forces with the Union Summer participants and campus labor activists around the country. The idea behind the campaign was simple: the overwhelming prevalence of sweatshops in the garment industry could be stopped. Students targeted the universities who directly profit from the exploitation of the women and men around the globe who made their clothes that bear the university logo. To stop this cycle of indignity, students began to demand that their universities take responsibility for the conditions under which their licensed apparel was made by adopting Codes of Conduct to regulate the behavior of their manufacturers. Over 200 college campuses eventually joined the fight and these students were successful in dozens of cases.

Youth Activist Step #5
Recruit Your Friends

An international movement paramount to ending slave labor was started by a bunch of photocopying interns. Get your friends on board, make new friends, and don't fight these battles alone.

Globalization

If Austin Powers represents internationalism, then globalization is Dr. Evil. They may look alike, but they are very different. Globalization is the brother with neither parent nor discipline, and no controlling authority to stop it from imposing its will on poorer nations, or teach it to respect the environment

---

[106] For example, many of us were upset by the Security Council before the war in Iraq, but, "61% of college students believe that the UN should play the major role in rebuilding Iraq with US Assistance and only 36% believed the US should take the lead. 41% of the general population supported a UN led effort and 54% supported a US led effort." Clearly we support the UN at a much higher rate. According to *CampusKids*.

and value its workers. In the 1990s, international workers and groups opposed to the unchecked growth of the International Monetary Fund (IMF) and World Trade Organization (WTO) found common cause with sympathetic college students. This coalition understood the potential for positive international development, but realized it would not come unless these International Governmental Organizations (IGOs) became more accountable.

"Many students make the connection that globalization is neither of, for, nor by the people and hence, they both resist it and resist being associated with it through monetary and trade policies at the federal level."[107] IGO distrust quickly spread suspicion of international corporations. Activists have criticized companies like Starbucks, Citigroup, and Nike for unjust overseas practices (usually egregious labor or environmental problems). Many Millennials rallied against "corporations of mass destruction." College students took aim at their alma maters and used "direct action"[108] to protest the fact that the popular athletic apparel was made overseas with sweatshop labor. These movements have been successful and we are now much more likely to wear clothing with University logos than corporate swooshes.

The success of the United Students Against Sweatshops (USAS) campaign spread to other types of college and youth activism and a few years later the best-known youth protest against globalization occurred at the "Battle in Seattle" in late

---

[107] NewStudentPolitics, p. 6.
[108] Direct Action, as defined in the Future500 means: "A strategy to raise issues or injustices through an individual or group's physical presence or collective activity. Show up at the Mayor's office, boycott a product, occupy and administrative building, flood a company with calls, faxes, or emails, create a mural without a permit, etc. Frequently involves a civil disobedience component, which entails breaking a law or an ordinance that is deemed unjust."

November 1999. Tens of thousands of people marched in a blue-green alliance of labor and environmentalists. Teamsters and turtle-lovers surprised the world with their strength and willingness to fight for global justice. The violence in Seattle is not what any of us wanted, but the birth of a movement is what some seeked to achieve.

Seattle, just the beginning, was a small part of a much larger global effort. Anti-globalization protests grew in the late 1990s and by October of 2001, Millennials were ready to converge on Washington in record numbers for the IMF/World Bank meetings. The city responded by planning to build a two million dollar, 14,000-foot chain-link fence around 220 downtown acres of the capitol.[109] George Washington University made arrangements to kick students out of the dorms and the city was ready for lockdown. As New York police prepared to join their brothers in blue in the nation's capitol, a showdown was in the making. Then September 11th happened. Protests, meetings, and police walls were all cancelled or scaled down for October as the world entered a new phase.

However, even after 9-11, these activists of our generation continued to march, and often messages of globalization, the impending invasion of Iraq, and civil liberties were mixed into one event. What the ANSWER Coalition,[110] Just Act,[111] and like-minded groups lacked in clarity they made up for in energy.

The scope of these marches is impressive. The *international*, anti-globalization movement combined with the protests against the war in Iraq is the largest since the Boomer

---

[109] Santana, Arthur and Manny Fernandez "DC Braces for IMF Protests." *WashPost* 07/10/01, p. B01.

[110] The ANSWER Coalition stands for Act Now to Stop War and End Racism. This group is responsible for most of the large anti war rallies in America. See: internationalanswer.org.

[111] Just Act, Youth Action for Global Justice, fights for social, economic and environmental justice. See: justact.org.

generation, Vietnam War protests of the '60s and '70s.[112] Also quite notable is the level of diversity in ethnicity and age that exists at these events, which was not as evident forty years earlier. However, despite the size of these marches, one cannot help but wonder if an "activist gap" is evolving similar to the "service gap" defined by United Leaders. As a generation we appear to be willing to march for or against a cause, but not always willing to vote for the folks who make the decisions. The 2002 UCLA/HERI survey showed that a record-high 47.5 percent of college freshman participated in organized demonstrations – not all of those people are voting though. Taking to the streets satisfies an emotional desire to advocate for social change, but intellectually we must connect our service and our activism to our politics to be successful in the long run. This is beginning to change, and only as we close these gaps will our generation begin to shape our country in lasting and profound ways.

It is also important to note that the media often missed the story at these rallies by focusing on the one teen with a rock rather than the hundreds of kids with signs. However, even if the entire world isn't noticing yet, the activism of our generation has certainly begun. One third of college students have participated in some type of political rally or demonstration.[113]

Boycotts / Buycotts

We've also taken our activism to the marketplace. For decades, activists used the power of the boycott to sway countries and companies, and Gen X deserves credit for their

---

[112] The size, and links to, the international wing of this movement is what most separates the current activism from the Vietnam era, but also according to the Washington Post, the 100,000+ protestors in D.C. in the fall of 2002 were "the largest since the Vietnam era." When the number of people in these domestic marches are added to the international populations marching the numbers add up quickly. This is particularly interesting since the Vietnam War lasted almost twenty years and the war in Iraq about twenty days. Reel, Monte and Manny Fernandez. "100,000 Rally, March Against War in Iraq." *WashPost*, 10/27/02, p. A01

[113] *CampusKids*, p 2.

role in boycotting companies that did business in South Africa to end apartheid.[114] But Millennials are taking it a step further with the "buycott." Since we have such economic power, we are not only boycotting those companies we disapprove of, but also buycotting that which we do approve of – "reward and punish" is the mantra of this economic activism.

One youth activist group, the United Students for Fair Trade, is educating Millennials about fair trade coffee and trying to create a demand on college campuses and across the country for the moral coffee bean. Starbucks often the poster child for our chain restaurant, consumer society has taken the step to sell fair trade coffee as an option in all of their stores. For only a few cents more, your $3.58 double caramel mocha latte will not only satisfy your caffeine addiction and your sweet tooth, but also your moral compass. We recognize this as a positive development for Starbucks, but also remember that it runs the risk of being a band-aid solution to quiet criticism rather than the first step in changing a global problem. We must use our economic strength and vote with our wallets and our ballots when given the option.

International Service

Millennials are certainly protesting globalization on college campuses and in their buying habits; but we remain an international generation. Youth international volunteerism has been on the rise with government programs like the Peace Corps expanding and new international non-profits proliferating.

Youth Activism Resource: Taking It Global (TIG)
TIG fosters a sense of leadership and social entrepreneurship through an innovative use of technology. The website is a wonderful resource for activist to learn new ideas, network with others, and to make their voice heard.
www.takingitglobal.org

---

[114] Apartheid was a political system in South Africa that institutionalized racism. It ended in 1994.

From the American Anti-Slavery Group to Students for a Free Tibet, we've been very active in international service organizations fighting for international justice. Many Millennials have started international nonprofits to promote change. In 1997, Global Youth Connect was started by young people who were intent on finding new ways to prevent the crimes against humanity ravaging the former Yugoslavia, Rwanda and other parts of the world. These international young activists wanted to build an organization that would prevent these atrocities from happening in the first place.

Michael Furdyk and Jennifer Corriero – and their site takingitglobal.org – are perhaps the best examples of the international service movement. Led by youth and empowered by technology, TIG brings together young people from over 215 countries in an active online community dedicated to inspiring, empowering and connecting young people to change the world. These two Canadians and 15,000 of their friends are changing the world.

Benjamin Quinto, Director of the Global Youth Action Network, is mobilizing tens of thousands of Millennials. The GYAN is an international collaboration among youth and youth-serving organizations to share information, resources and solutions. Its purpose is to promote greater youth engagement. Benjamin wasn't old enough to drive when he began to develop a proposal for a permanent body of youth to work in cooperation with the United Nations. He worked for three and half years on what became the Global Youth Assembly Project. Today, Benjamin still runs GYAN and works with TIG towards his vision of a unified international youth movement.

Working closely with Ben is Jonah Wittkamper who reminds the world, "When Einstein passed away he recommended two strategies for solving global problems: a world youth parliament and a global spirituality." According to Jonah the United Nations suffers from a democratic deficit and needs a boost of youth and citizen participation for greater legitimacy. He has spent several years researching the role and need for youth participation in global decision-making and argues that in order to create a Parliament or permanent global structure for youth a number of supporting structures are needed such as 1) a global network of local youth networks, 2) a federation of global youth networks, 3) a consolidated communication system among them, 4) international standards for youth participation in global decision-making forums, and 5) a watch dog system to defend youth from tokenization in such forums.[115]

International Economic Forces

Finally, Millennials are moving into careers in international business as well. Remember, the vast majority of us are *not* anti-capitalist. Millennials like Chris Landon from Old Brookville, New York moved to Argentina to work in Buenos Aires for Prudential Securities. Like thousands before him, Chris started in a desk job in New York City, but when his boss found out that this Caucasian Catholic was also fluent in Spanish, he found himself headed to South America. And when world-traveling Millennials like Chris end up moving back home, they are likely to bring home spouses from foreign lands, further intensifying the internationalism of our generation.

For many of us, our capitalism is not divorced from our activism. The idea of a global communist order has been dead since our birth and we've grown up seeing the direct correlation between capitalism, democracy and human freedom. Free markets mean free people; no two countries with McDonalds have ever fought a war against each other.[116] We will continue this trend, and in particular make sure that we promote a democratic capitalism rather than an imperialist one. A capitalism that respects human rights and the environment, that

---

[115] See: youthmovements.org/comp.htm p. 8. Viewed on 06/10/03.
[116] Bagby, Meredith. We've Got Issues. p. 266.

has limits to greed, and one where innovative entrepreneurs of any race or economic class can earn incredible wealth.

Global Millennials

Internationalism is such a big part of this generation, and Americanism is such an important part of young people around the world. This unique situation has caused some people to predict the emergence of a global generation. The first uniform global generation will evolve when entire cohorts of young people are affected by the same events in similar ways at the same time. This is not the case for Millennials. Despite near universal awareness of news from DC to Hollywood, the world's youth are not responding to these events in likeminded ways. September 11th came close with nearly a world wide show of sympathy and unity with the United States, but less than two years later it became clear that even Europe is not politically unified, much less the world.

However, with nearly half of all people in the world today under the age of 25,[117] and with these young people more connected than ever before, people our age will be faced with solving the world's problems sooner than later. Hopefully, we'll be solving these problems together rather than creating new ones.

---

[117] Montgomery, Cherreka. "The Critical Role of Youth in Global Development." Issue Brief 12/01. Washington, DC: International Center for Research on Women, 2001. p. 1.

"Yes, I believe." *Cassie Bernall,*
Columbine Junior who was killed after professing her faith.

6

RENDER UNTO CAESAR

Gen Xers were not only infamous for turning away from politics, but also for turning away from other traditional institutions like family, civic organizations, and religion. According to Robert Putnam, our whole society was bowling alone. However, Millennials have reversed that trend, especially with religion, and led a visible revival among youth religious groups, high school bible studies, and the discussion of spirituality on college campuses.[118] This return to faith shapes our social and political attitudes a great deal, especially when many of the most contentious issues in society (such as the death penalty, cloning and abortion) have a critical element of morality in them. One of the most common misunderstandings when it comes to our generation is that we have no faith. However, especially in our politics, *religion matters a great deal.* Millennials do not all have religious beliefs, nor do we think uniformly when it comes to these issues, but on the whole we appreciate our own religious background and understand that it is important to many of our peers.

We have found when reading books about politics that most of them either don't address the issue of religion and values, or that's all they address. However, the religious revival among our generation and the current revolution in the role of "Church and

---

[118] In Millennials Rising, Strauss and Howe point out that "55% of teens go to church regularly versus 45% of Americans as a whole," p. 234.

State" begs for analysis. What role does religion play in shaping our generation's activism?

Many adults are surprised when they learn more about this issue. All across this country, in public, private and charter schools, religion is in the schools. "In 1990, there were no prayer circles or clubs in U.S. public high schools, now there are 10,000 of them."[119] Football players are praying before each game and after each touchdown. Peer counseling groups are using religion with reflection and faith with fellowship to help other students who are struggling through teenage years. Cool kids are partying on Saturday night and attending Bible studies on Sunday. Eighty-three percent of college freshman occasionally attend religious services, up from 75 percent in 1983.[120] Even kindergarten students are saying grace before snack time.[121] We are not the "organizational generation" as driven to succeed and devoid of faith as some of our parents would suggest.[122]

While every Millennial is not wearing a WWJD bracelet, we all know that it stands for "What Would Jesus Do?" Religion is debated, discussed, investigated, explored, questioned and celebrated. We are not turning away from the church due to doubt of the

> **Youth Activism Resource: Campus Compact**
>
> Campus Compact is a national coalition of close to 850 college and university presidents committed to the civic purposes of higher education. To support this civic mission, Campus Compact promotes community service that develops students' citizenship skills and values, encourages partnerships between campuses and communities, and assists faculty who seek to integrate public and community engagement into their teaching and research.
>
> www.compact.org

---

[119] Howe and Strauss, Millennials Rising, p.234
[120] *UCLA/HERI* Information from *Millennials2College*, p. 8.
[121] "The Rutherford Institute Wins Victory for Kindergartner Prevented from Saying Grace Before Snack Time" Rutherford Institute Press Release, 06/10/2002.
[122] David Brooks wrote an article in the 4/00 Atlantic Monthly suggesting just that.

deity or distrust of the institutions; instead we are changing the church by modernizing its values. According to Reverend Parent, a priest who recruits for the Catholic Church, "[Recruitment is up] and 'the millennial generation' seems to be less cynical and more open to traditional institutions than the Gen Xers and boomers."[123] Again, much like the personal nature of political scandals makes us question politicians and not the system, so too with the Catholic Church and other religious scandals. The failings of priests make us question priests, not God.

Genetic Engineering

There are incredible moral decisions on the horizon that society must make about the realistic possibility of cloning humans and the frightening potential of genetic discrimination. Science offers hope in curing life-threatening diseases, but when scientists predict they can cure "shyness" in less than ten years, it must prompt us to examine what our values are. We must examine the religious and social consequences of some scientific choices.

While faith is an important part of the generation, we are not luddites. Advances in science have lengthened life spans and made us healthier while living. Our generation won't violently resist the genetic engineering of plants because we know how powerful the positive changes can be. However, those powerful changes may have unintended environmental and health consequences. We will continue to demand that science proceed with caution as discoveries modify nature at speeds more rapidly than even before.

When you move beyond plants, the morality of genetic engineering gets tricky. While conservatives and liberals have begun to find common ground on stem cell research, this is just

---

[123] McCombs, Phil. "A Few Very Good Men" *WashPost*, 06/09/02, p. F01

the tip of the iceberg. Science fiction is rapidly becoming science fact and our generation possesses the realistic potential to modify our children in the future.

If the science is available to make our babies smarter, healthier, and stronger, would we deny them that potential? What if other countries began to change their children? Will it become an issue of national security? Current political and moral leaders condemn such practices, but our generation won't be so quick to judgment.

Genetic engineering is not the only way we will have the potential to change the human race. Advances in robotics being integrated into living beings could change us all. For well over a decade, pacemakers have kept our hearts beating on time, but what will come in the next ten years? Will the paralyzed walk? Will our brains be Internet enabled? It was amazing enough when Sony turned a robot into a soccer-playing dog, but now the military has created mind and body-controlling devices to turn rats into robots.[124] Are monkeys or humans far behind?

Church and State

This is another issue that is radicalized by our Boomer parents. Schools should not be tools of religion or of atheism; they should be institutions of learning. Instead of the Ten Commandments let us post honor codes. Instead of ending school prayer, how about moments of silence in the classroom. After-school Bible studies should be allowed to use school space if they are after hours and all faiths are permitted. We don't need to remove God from the Pledge of Allegiance or take Christ out of Christmas.

To make people of all religions comfortable, many schools today are excluding of all expressions of faith. At Columbine,

---

[124] The US Military has been able to connect mind-controlling machines to rats to control their movement, possibly as a tool for intelligence gathering, defusing bombs, and more. See: news.nationalgeographic.com/news/2002/05/0501_020501_roborats.html.

students were given an opportunity to make tiles to commemorate the loss of their classmates. When many students put religious messages on these plates, they were barred from being included in the memorial – despite the professed faith of some of the fallen students. We need an inclusive system, which does not favor any one religion.

Millennials are moderates looking for solutions that neither divorce religion from schools nor impose community religious values on others. Education policy should be set and implemented locally, but this is one issue where the federal government needs to give more guidance to help strike a healthy balance of a logical, constitutional separation of church and state without irrational barriers between faith and daily life.

Case Study: New Light Leadership Coalition (NLLC)
November 13, 1999 a group of African American teenagers organized the Youth Summit '99, "Preparing to Rule: Leaders of the New Millennium" at Frederick Douglas High School in Baltimore, Maryland. At this conference they involved the Maryland State Election Board, Howard University, and Black Entertainment Television (BET). They included African dance, hip hop, drama, and poetry to have some fun. The event was so successful that the next year they grew into the Baltimore Convention Center and involved hundreds more young people. In November of 2004 they will have their sixth annual conference for youth around the country.

Youth Activist Step #6
Get Organized
The NLLC broke down into a number of committees and recruited the help of many people. Through a well-organized web site, email lists and school meetings, they were able to prepare for their first event and to grow after early success.

The Death Penalty
With the election of George W. Bush and the appointment of John Ashcroft as Attorney General, capital punishment began to

take center stage. According to Gallup, "younger Americans – those under thirty years old – are somewhat less likely to favor the death penalty than older Americans."[125] A majority of our generation supports the *idea* of the death penalty (in concept, there are some crimes which rise to the level of the death penalty), and a smaller majority supports the *actual system* of punishment (in reality, this system of punishment is enforced by humans who are not perfect). Our generation has a healthy level of skepticism of a system that has put innocent people on death row, ended the lives of the mentally ill, and is in violation of the U.N. Universal Declaration of Human Rights. However, most of us do believe a person who is truly guilty of certain heinous crimes is not above being put to death.

The death penalty is an issue that national leaders of both parties don't seem willing to debate. Presidents Reagan, Bush and Clinton were all in favor of capital punishment, so national debate on this subject has been limited during our lifetime. But Millennials may begin to change that, especially as it starts to hit home. "There were as many executions of juvenile offenders in the U.S. in the year 2000 as there were in the previous six years combined."[126] In the 2000 National Youth Platform, Millennials went as far as to say, "the death penalty is no longer merely a form of punishment; rather it is a form of cruel and unusual punishment as prohibited by the Fifth Amendment of the Constitution." These young leaders are slightly ahead of the curve of the rest of the generation, but could be a clear indicator of things to come.

Surprisingly, as this debate develops it will not just take on moral tones. Practical arguments against an imperfect system

---

[125] "The latest poll shows support [for the death penalty] among older Americans around 70%, while support among those under 30 is in the low 60s." Jones, Jeffery M. "Two thirds of Americans support the death penalty." *Gallup*, 03/02/01. See: gallup.com/poll/releases/pr010301.asp.

[126] Hughes, Della, Miriam Rollin and Cassandra McKee, "2001 Advocacy Kit." Washington, DC, National Network for Youth, 2001. p. JJDPA-5. (a.k.a *NNYKit*)

and international pressure may lead to the end of the death penalty. If you look at the countries that currently allow the death penalty, it is a who's who of the axis of evil and the United States.[127] No European Union nation allows for capital punishment. It certainly remains unclear whether we, as a generation, will completely eliminate capital punishment, but there are certainly signs that we'll advocate for far less common use of the practice.

Abortion

Millennials generally rank abortion lower on the "most important issue" list than older conservatives and liberals. In one 2000 national survey of youth, abortion came up thirteenth out of sixteen top issues affecting our country. It didn't even make the list for top issues affecting the generation![128] There is a reason for that. Generally Millennials are in favor of current laws and don't think they'll change any time soon. Liberals argue we take for granted the rights won by former activists and conservatives condemn youth for not valuing human life.

However, Millennials are less supportive of abortion than previous generations. "Prior to the *Roe v. Wade* decision in 1973, nearly 86 percent of the students said abortion should be legalized. Many who were college freshmen in 1970 now have their own children attending college. In 2002, a little more than 53 percent said abortion should be legal."[129] In 2003, Gallup Youth Survey found "that while a majority of teens (aged thirteen to seventeen) do find abortion acceptable, a full third believe that it should be illegal in all circumstances. Approximately one-fifth of teens support the legality of abortion

---

[127] Iraq, Iran, North Korea, China, Pakistan, Syria, Sudan, Somalia and the U.S. are among the only 31 out of 193 sovereign nations in the world that used the death penalty in 2002.

[128] *NatYouthSurvey2000.*

[129] Bluey, Robert B. "Youth Attitudes on Abortion Encourage Pro-Life Groups" CNSNews Service, 04/06/03.

under any circumstances, while twice that number believe it should be legal only under certain circumstances."[130] The numbers get a little confusing, but what is most important to remember is that our faith is influencing our politics. According to Sara McKalips, the assistant director of Rock for Life, "They [Millennials] don't see abortion as just a women's rights issue, they also see it now as a human rights issue."[131]

The majority of Millennials greatly value the potential of life and want to see fewer abortions, but without more laws imposed that risk moving the procedure from the doctor's offices to the back alleys. Although more divided than previous generations over abortion,[132] we hope the issue will be less polarizing in future American politics since it is not a dominant political priority for most of us.

Religious Activism

Just like young people who are in political parties or ethnic organizations vote at a higher rate and are more politically engaged, the same is true with religious youth too. Young churchgoers see political participation as meaningful. Nearly two-thirds of devout young adults (64%) say voting is extremely or very important, compared to about one-third (37%) of non-churchgoers.[133] A large number of us are even volunteering with faith-based organizations. According to David Gergen, "One in seven AmeriCorps members are now serving in faith-based projects."[134]

Organizations like the National Catholic Youth, Christian Coalition, Hillel, Kadima, Unitarian United, Latter-Day Saints, Bahai Youth, and the National Muslim Students Association

[130] *Gallup.*
[131] Bluey, Robert B. "Youth Attitudes on Abortion Encourage Pro-Life Groups" CNSNews Service, 04/06/03.
[132] Bowman, Karlyn. "Abortion Attitudes Today." *Gallup*, 01/00. See: gallup.com/poll/guest_scholar/gs000112.asp. Viewed on 06/01/03.
[133] *TrustMatters*, p. 35.
[134] Gergen, David. "The Nation's New Patriots. *USNews*, 11/2/98. p. 68.

(among many) have had youth participation grow over the last ten years and are increasingly willing to blend religious activism with civic engagement.[135] As more and more political issues take moral tones this is sure to increasingly shape our generation's politics.

Cultural Conservatism

Culturally we are more conservative, traditional, and modest than Gen Xers or Boomers. According to Strauss and Howe, "When Millennial teens are asked to identify 'the major causes' of America's problems, their seven most popular answers all pertain to what they perceive as excess of adult individualism. Reason number one (given by 56 percent of all teens) is 'selfishness, people not thinking of the rights of others.' Reason number two (given by 52 percent) is 'people who don't respect the law and the authorities.'"[136] We as a generation are sick of a society that puts corporate interests, over individual wants, over community needs. We are ready to turn all of that around.

Pollster George Gallup, Jr. described us this way: "Teens today are decidedly more traditional than their parents were, in both life-styles and attitudes. Gallup Youth Survey data from the past 25 years reveals that teens today are far less likely than their parents were to use alcohol, tobacco, and marijuana. In addition, they are less likely than their parents even today to approve of sex before marriage and having children out of wedlock. Teens want to reduce the amount of violence on TV; seek clear rules to live by, and promote the teaching of values in school. They are searching for religion and spiritual moorings in

---

[135] For example, "More than 17,000 high schoolers attended the National Catholic Youth conference in 1997, up from 7,000 in 1993. Membership in Kadima, the conservative Jewish organization for middle school kids, stands at the highest level ever." From Howe and Strauss, Millennials Rising, p. 236.

[136] *Millennials2College*, p. 36.

their lives. They want abstinence taught in school, and they think divorces should be harder to get."[137]

The progress our generation has made in reducing teen pregnancy is the perfect example. While popular culture and may portray youth as sexually liberal, teen pregnancy has been on an eleven year decline. According to the National Center for Health Statistics, the teen birth rate fell to 43 births per 1,000 females aged 15-19, a record low. These new figures represent a 28 percent decline from 1990.

We are not the misbehaving, dumb kids that Hollywood and the media make us out to be. We're quite well behaved and our cultural conservatism is an important part of our view of government. Our generation is defining a new kind of politics. Soon people will realize that we don't fit neatly in prepackaged political parties of the 20th century.

---

[137] *Millennials2College*, p. 37.

"Days after taking office, [Attorney General John Ashcroft] vowed on *Larry King Live* to 'escalate the war on drugs . . . relaunch it if you will.' But he said, 'I think we've got enough laws on the books [for guns].'" – *Evan Gahr* [138]

7

PLAYING WITH FIRE

On April 20, 1999 two Millennials stormed Columbine High School and shot and killed twelve of their fellow classmates, a teacher, and eventually themselves. Before September 11th, this day was our generation's "assassination of President Kennedy." We all know where we were and what we were doing when Eric Harris and Dylan Klebold made us fear going to school. This day will forever be in the minds of Millennials when it comes to gun control. In fact, gun control is one of the few political issues where a true generational consensus can be found. This debate started over a century ago, but will soon be resolved when Millennials are in charge of the government.

After guns, there are few political issues in our country that have become more polarized and misrepresented by politicians, the media and special interests than the issue of drugs. We are a drugged-up generation, filled to the eyelids with Ritalin while being told that ecstasy may kill you if you get too dehydrated. Our ADD minds can concentrate long enough to recognize that this is crazy talk. With the failing "War on Drugs," a number of people in our generation feel as if we need to reduce the rhetoric

---

[138] Gahr, Evan. "Fellow Conservatives: Our Position Is Hypocritical." *WashPost*, 04/22/01, p. B03.

and begin finding compromise solutions that re-examine our current approach to drug and alcohol policy.

Guns

Youth-led gun control organizations were created all over the country after Columbine and continue to be supported by organizations like the Alliance for Justice.[139] However, don't be fooled into thinking Millennials are raging liberals on the issue of guns. We don't want liberal Michael Moore or conservative Charleston Heston writing our gun laws. We believe there is a huge middle road that we should follow.

Case Study: Kidz Voice-LA

Theo and Nick Milonopoulous, twin brothers from Los Angeles, co-founded Kidz Voice-LA when they were twelve years old to address the issues of gun violence. In Los Angeles there were 150 young people shot in 1998, 53 of them fatal. Through petitions, attendance at anti-gun violence marches and public speeches, Theo and Nick helped change the city's gun policy. In April 2001, they successfully lobbied the City Council to pass a partial ban on ammunition sales. On National Youth Service Day 2002, Kidz Voice-LA led a "Get Out the Vote" campaign and distributed 300 bilingual voter registration forms for the city's election.

Youth Activist Step #7
Build Your Coalition
Kidz Voice succeeded with support from city, county, and state legislators, gun-control organizations, student councils, and parent-teacher organizations.

The Kaiser Family Foundation found Millennials "favor tougher gun control – 84 percent support mandatory waiting periods and criminal background checks."[140] Gun control is more than a generational issue – it is also a regional issue. Citizens of all ages tend to support gun control more in urban and suburban areas and less in

---

[139] The Alliance for Justice Co-Motion program provides money and support to young activists addressing the issue of guns. See: afj.org.
[140] According to *KFFSurvey*.

rural areas. This makes gun ownership more acceptable in those societies and often something that is passed down from generation to generation. However, the rural influence on this debate is increasingly less important as more urban migration has undercut the traditional gun owner's base. Many urban Millennials are in favor of gun rights to protect themselves on the mean streets of the cities, but these urban youth do not have the same passion for gun rights as do young hunters and sportsmen do in rural areas.

There are many Millennials who are a part of the National Rifle Association (NRA). Sometimes more moderate than the current leadership, these conservative believe that it is not the guns that are harming our society, but rather the lack of awareness and education that surround their use. To fix this problem the NRA partners with organizations like the Boy Scouts of America, American Legion, and 4-H Clubs. In addition to education, many young conservatives believe enforcement of current laws is more important than new laws; but we must make sure this enforcement is funded by Congress to get illegal guns off the street.

However, Millennials generally favor gun control more than other generations, and they are also less interested in guns for sport. There is more competition to entertain young people these days than hunting deer. As kids, we played with soccer balls, not BB guns. More of us are playing organized sports, surfing the Net, and playing video games.

Many people in the gun control movement believe they are on the brink of winning the war, and that within the next decade gun control will be completely accepted in society and no longer debated every year in Congress. There will always be hunters and sportsmen, but in the future the National Rifle Association (NRA) will not be one of the most powerful lobbying organizations in the country; criminals will not be able to buy guns through any gun show loopholes; waiting periods will be fast and effective; safety locks will be required; and, guns will leave fingerprints on the bullets they fire. With common sense laws, guns will always be available for hunters, sportsmen, and law-abiding citizens without criminal records. Millennials are not outliers on this issue. An overwhelming majority of Americans support both regulating the gun industry and licensing and registration of gun owners. "A Gallup poll taken just two weeks before the [2000] elections revealed that 77 percent of Americans support handgun owner licensing. And CNN Election Day exit polls showed a full 60 percent of voters favoring stronger gun control laws."[141] Since the 2000 Election, 9-11 and the DC sniper have magnified these views. These polls indicate there *is* an American gun consensus.

INTERESTING GUN FACTS

About 30,000 people in America die every year from firearms-related injuries. Gun control advocates point out that the rate of firearm deaths among children fourteen years and younger is nearly twelve times higher than in 25 industrialized countries combined.[142]

America's most comprehensive gun control legislation passed in 1993. While fatalities fell more than 25 percent from '93 to '98, the drop in gun-related injuries is even more telling - down nearly 50 percent, to 23.9 per 100,000, in the same time period. And that reduction spans all three major categories - assault, accidental and intentional self-infliction.[143]

Drugs

In addition to the mistakes that the government has made with respect to gun policy, it has also misallocated time, energy and money on the war on drugs. "The cost of imprisoning one person for one year is close to $30,000, while the cost for

---

[141] Beard, Michael K. "Regulate Gun Purchasers or the Gun Industry?" Coalition to Stop Gun Violence, Media Release 04/20/01.

[142] Pleming, Sue. "Gun Control Lobby Urges Congress to Act." *Reuters*, 04/19/01. See: vikingphoenix.com/news/archives/2001/fa/fa2001-025.htm

[143] CDC, 04/12/01. Analysts at the CDC released some fascinating figures on gun-related crime from 1993 through 1998.

rehabilitative treatment in a methadone clinic for one year is $4,000."[144] The government has focused on spending money on propaganda rather than research, and energy on penalizing small criminals rather than reforming individuals with addictions. Further, the way society has embraced certain legal drugs to solve arguably normal childhood behavior without knowing the long-term consequences cries out for attention.

We have so many questions about America's drug policy – it just doesn't make any sense! People with minor drug convictions need to be reformed, not cast aside and thrown in prison. Very few of them are a major threat to society. Why are people with drug convictions ineligible for

> **Youth Activism Resource:**
> **ShiNE: Seeking Harmony In**
> **Neighborhoods Everyday**
> ShiNE works to improve teens' lives by helping build self-esteem, foster nonviolence and respect for diversity and promote youth leadership. ShiNE teaches teens to use technology and provides them the tools to advance social causes.
> www.shine.com

federal financial aid for college,[145] but people with a history of sexual offenses are still eligible? Why does crack cocaine, a typically "black" drug, carry much harsher penalties than powdered cocaine, a typically rich "white" drug?[146] Is the four million dollars the American taxpayer paid for "Plan Columbia"[147] a good idea? Why does the federal government stop states and doctors from allowing marijuana to be used for medical reasons? Given that some research "suggests that [Ritalin] has the potential for causing long-lasting changes in

---

[144] *NYP 2000*, p 9.
[145] The Drug-Free Student Aid Provision prevents kids who have ever been arrested or convicted of a drug-related offense from getting federal financial aid for college.
[146] "The amount of crack you need to get a five-year mandatory minimum is 5 grams, but for powder cocaine its 500 grams – which is interesting once you learn that 75% of those arrested for powder cocaine are white, and 90% of those arrested for crack are African-American." Wimsatt, William. No More Prisons, p 9.
[147] According to the *Future500*: Plan Columbia is "a $4 million 'aid package' to the Columbian military to fight the drug war that has been linked with paramilitary death squads, torture, and indiscriminate fumigation of crops."

brain cell structure and function,"[148] is dope less dangerous that Ritalin?

In Canada, inconsistencies in drug laws have led the courts to push the government to decriminalize weed. In America, all we're asking for is an honest broker to evaluate the effect of illegal drugs on people and the effect of drug policy on drug use. According to the University of Michigan, 37 percent of high school seniors told researchers that they had smoked pot within the previous twelve months; 8.2 percent had used the stimulant Ecstasy within the previous twelve months;[149] and 20 percent had had used other illicit drugs like cocaine or heroin in the past year.[150] If one-third of our generation is using drugs, then we need some real answers, especially if drug users are unnecessarily flooding our prisons. We are not crazy druggies, "sixty-one percent of college students oppose legalizing marijuana."[151] But, there is a significant difference between legalizing (removing all laws) and decriminalizing (*significantly* reducing those laws) for many Millennials. Furthermore, opposition to legalization has been on a two-decade decline.[152] Stay tuned; this is one debate that we believe we will resolve in the next decade. The demand for honest research will be answered and just as the Soviet Union folded under the expense of the Cold War, our nation will demand changes as the price tag on the War on Drugs continues to climb.

Alcohol and Tobacco

Although legal, both of these drugs play an important role in our generation. Lawsuits by states against tobacco companies led to a huge settlement that, among other things, funds "The Truth"

[148] Brennan, Cory. "Parents, Educators Fight 'Legal' Drugs in Schools" *Freedom Magazine*, 4/25/03. freedommag.org/english/Press/page06.htm
[149] Gahr, Evan. Ibid, p. B03
[150] Winter, Greg. "Study Finds No Sign That Testing Deters Students' Drug Use." *NYTimes*, 3/17/03, p, 1A.
[151] *CampusKids.*
[152] *Millennials2College*, p. 34.

campaign. No fifty-year-old, wrinkled faced, one-lung Millennial will ever be able to claim that they didn't know battery acid was in their Marlboro Man: the truth is out there. Generally, Millennials are in favor of stricter tobacco laws such as those in states like California and Delaware, which limit second hand smoke but don't outlaw private use. Millennials are typically not in favor of laws like the one New Jersey considered to raise the legal smoking age to twenty-one.[153] A law like this may have the opposite effect of the intent of the bill by making tobacco a forbidden fruit that is cool for secret use. Millennials are particularly supportive of information campaigns geared towards young people. However, some campaigns verge on propaganda and can have the reverse effect on smoking trends. Many of us may be anti-corporate, but that does not go as far as abdicating individuals from their own personal responsibility and letting trials lawyers clean up all of our personal mistakes.

In Utah, the Provo High School Self Esteem Club pursued the idea of a Clean Indoor Air Law and mobilized students from more than twenty high schools across the state. Over 2000 students came to the rally at the State Capitol. Despite overwhelming opposition from the state's restaurant and tourism industry, the Clean Indoor Air Law passed.[154] The American Legacy Foundation, those guys who do The Truth campaign, also supports youth activism groups like the Provo High club.

Despite what you see in the papers, we are not drinking as much alcohol and liquor as previous generations did.[155] Despite reduced use, however, we feel that alcohol laws are not working and have an absurd effect on our generation. We've seen brilliant minds in our generation drink themselves blind in high school and college before it was legal to drink. Women raped, young men died, and riots occurred in part because alcohol is a

---

[153] "Two NJ lawmakers want to raise age to buy cigarettes." *AP*, 4/25/03.
[154] *Project540*, p. 67.
[155] "Alcohol use has declined precipitously since the late 1980s: from 65.8% to 52.6% for beer drinking and 66.7% to 54.9% for wine or liquor." *HERI/UCLA 30yr*, p. 30.

forbidden fruit that we don't learn how to control growing up. Some Millennials believe we need a graduated system that teaches responsible drinking at home and slowly increases rights with age. These Millennials believe that this type of system would show that liquor itself is neither good nor bad, but that it must be used properly and responsibly. Further it would end the quiet discrimination against ethnic and religious traditions that involve alcohol (usually wine), even for those under eighteen.

Prisons

Next time you are in a major city, take a break from looking up at the skyscrapers of New York or Chicago, the monuments in Washington, or the models in LA or Miami and look down at your feet. Spray-painted on sidewalks across this country, you'll read "No More Prisons." This is the title of an outstanding book on youth activism by Billy "Upski" Wimsatt and the theme of an urban youth movement to empower our generation bring attention to the growing prison-industrial complex.

Billy points out early in his book that sixty percent of all prisoners are incarcerated for non-violent offenses. There are far too many people (including young people) in jail who don't deserve to be there. A Senate subcommittee took a national survey of prison wardens that found "ninety two percent of wardens believed that 'greater uses should be made of alternatives to incarceration ... [and that] on average half the offenders under their supervision could be released without endangering public

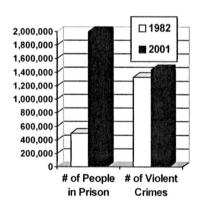

safety."[156] These guys seemed willing to talk themselves out of a job, or perhaps just willing to tell the honest truth.[157] Currently young people are being tried as adults at record numbers and juveniles are being put in adult jails. Youth who are locked in jails are at great risk for abuse. A fifteen-year-old girl in Ohio who ran away from home was put in the county jail because the judge wanted to 'teach her a lesson.' The deputy jailer then raped this girl. In Idaho, a seventeen-year-old boy who had not paid a $73 traffic fine was held in an adult jail where he was tortured and eventually murdered by the other prisoners in his cell.[158] Although extreme cases, both of these stories are true and shine a light on how horrific jails can be, especially for youth wrongly placed in adult jails. The solution to this problem is not building more youth jails, but more education for youth before they get into trouble and appropriate sentencing when mistakes are made.

Jails aren't just ageist, they're racist, too. Blacks and other minorities are disproportionately locked up, often cannot afford effective counsel, and are racially profiled every day. "One in seven black men are disenfranchised due to felony convictions. In sum, if there is any single area of American life that contributes to a continuing sense of racial discrimination, it is crime and the criminal justice system."[159]

Millennials are starting to fight back against the "prison industrial complex"[160] we see locking up our generation. In response to the Proposition 21 ballot initiative in California aimed to try fourteen-year-olds as adults and put sixteen year

---

[156] Wimsatt, William. No More Prisons, p. 8.
[157] Information from the prison chart came from the FBI Uniform Crime Reports, 2001. See: fbi.gov/ucr/cius_01/xl/01tbl01.xls
[158] *NNYKit*, p. 2JJDPA.
[159] *DivGen*, p. 33.
[160] This term, "Prison Industrial Complex" is defined in *Future500* as: "Prisons are businesses and many are owned and run like corporations. To make sure business keeps growing, you gotta have more and more workers, i.e. prisoners, so policy-makers, politicians, and the media work with corporations to create laws and conditions that will incarcerate more and more people."

olds in prisons, a number of youth groups rallied to fight the initiative. Let's Get Free is one organization launched in 2001 by working class youth of color in the San Francisco Bay area using hip hop to fight the growing criminal justice system. This group led a campaign to stop Alameda County from building one of the largest per capita juvenile halls in the country. They also made a twenty-minute documentary film called *Books Not Bars* to raise awareness about their issue.[161]

In San Francisco, thousands of students started walking out of their schools as early as 1998 protesting the building of jails. Chanting, "education not incarceration," over 2,000 students walked out in April of 1999 and again the next fall when 3,000 students joined the rallies.[162] The movement found its way to Oklahoma by 2002 as Millennials protested to teachers that their history books were literally becoming a part of history and the state's excessive spending on prisons and the consequences of mandatory minimum sentences were hurting their future.[163]

Across the coast, kids in New York City were rising up against being locked down, too. The Justice 4 Youth Coalition, a group of high school kids, college students, and formerly incarcerated youth and adults, is fighting to make sure that the city prioritizes education over incarceration. Despite the fact that juvenile crime has dropped 30 percent over the last decade and current facilities are operating under capacity, the city wants to spend $66 million for new jail cells for youth.[164] The problem is not just in big cities. In the small state of Delaware, it costs

[161] See: booksnotbars.org.
[162] See: lairdcarlson.com/celldoor/00103/Greene00103CriticalMove.htm.
[163] Interview by Scott Beale of Oklahoma students participating in Close Up at a speech in Washington, DC on 5/12/03.
[164] See: nomoreyouthjails.org/j4y.

more to send a kid to jail than it does college![165] This fact just makes you want to spray paint "No More Prisons" on sidewalks and billboards to make people aware of the issue!

With over 800 youth courts across the country, Millennials are already starting to find solutions to the problems of jails in our society. Youth courts empower local youth as justice advisors who review acknowledged offenses by their peers to decide on appropriate sentences. The Harlem Youth Court is one of these courts allowing young jurors to question their peers, understand their offenses, and respond appropriately to the misdeed that was committed.[166] These courts are particularly effective with youth drug crimes. We believe this approach is much more successful than mandatory minimum prison sentences.

This incarceration of our generation is so important that it is a constant agenda item at Millennial conferences across the country. In the spring 2003, at the Mobilizing America's Youth conference, juvenile justice was voted as one of the three most important issues for the generation. In 2000, the National Youth Platform also emphasized this issue: "The juvenile justice system must focus on helping young people become productive members of our society; it must not treat them as predators and write them off when they have an entire lifetime ahead of them. By changing the focus of the system from revenge to reform, we will eventually bring these young people into society as productive members."[167]

Make no mistake; we are not a generation soft on crime or so socially liberal as to embrace a free wheeling drug and alcohol culture. Millennials are quite socially conservative in many of

---

[165] Dodenhoff, Jennifer. "First Unitarian Church to Host Criminal Justice Reform Forum." *DE Citizens Opposed to the Death Penalty*, Email Announcement, 4/29/03.
[166] *Project540*, p. 51
[167] *NYP 2000*, p 10.

these areas. We use fewer hard drugs than Xers,[168] are more sexually conservative than past generations,[169] and seek to find opportunities for entertainment that don't involve liquor or pot. We are not trying to fight for a lascivious lifestyle; we're rationally looking for answers to problems that our parents have so poorly addressed. Don't expect us to use crack or smoke pot and then later champion zero-tolerance, zero-thought drug laws like some Boomer politicians. We want to fix this problem, not perpetuate it.

Ending the Wars

The statistics underestimate the political relevance of gun, drug, and prison issues amongst youth. We've interviewed thousands of Millennials and attended hundreds of conferences, and even among non-drug using youth, there is support for liberalizing the drug laws. Even among gun owning Millennials, there is support for laws that protect people (even hunters) and make life difficult for criminals. And the under-reported, but eminently visible, rise of prisons in our society offends all those who are aware of it.

Let's end the 20th century battles over drugs, guns and prisons; we have bigger wars to win and a battle for a better society to fight.

---

[168] In 1981, 30% of high school seniors used marijuana and 5% used cocaine. In 2001, 21% of high school seniors used marijuana and 2% used cocaine. According to the White House ONDCP, 10/02 Drug Use Trends. See: whitehousedrugpolicy.gov.
[169] "Support for 'causal sex' has declined from its high point of 51.9% in 1987 to 41.6% in 1996." *HERI/UCLA30yr*, p. 29.

"Blessed are the young, for they shall inherit the national debt." –
Herbert Hoover, Thirty-first President of the United States

8

WE THE PEOPLE

As discussed in Chapter Four, race still divides our country, but so does the issue of economic class. And while hundreds of non-profit groups, advocacy organizations, schools and government institutions are addressing the issue of race; it is considered un-American to talk about economic class. We have grown up on the popular misconception that we have a completely fluid class society – that anyone who is hard working can climb the social ladder and join the upper crust. While this is truer in America than in other nations, we all know that it is not completely true, and it is less true than it was even a few decades ago. (And it will be even further from reach in another decade if we don't do something about it.)

We believe that class divides Millennials at least as much as race does. Rich kids go to rich high schools, live in rich neighborhoods and attend rich colleges (and therefore date other rich people). While heavily correlated, race is a secondary issue in most areas of our lives. It is cool and sexy to date across racial lines; young people don't even talk about it. Even in our judicial system, class seems to come into play. Many of us believe that guilty or not, O.J. Simpson got off because he could afford the best lawyers. America's reaction to the case underscored racial divides in our society, but the verdict was determined much more by money than by skin color.

We raise the issue of class not because we are communist or anti-capitalist; we raise the issue of class because it is important to our generation and it is an issue that is on the rise. In a 2000 Oregon State University survey of youth nationwide, "homelessness/poverty" was rated the single most important issue facing our country.[170] As teens we created organizations like "Happy Helpers for the Homeless" [171] to feed the poor and the hungry. But we are no longer happy helpers making bag lunches; we are impatient citizens displeased with liberal and conservative non-solutions to the issue of poverty. "Most homeless people are under eighteen years of age, and we want to know how the 'richest nation in the world' accounts for the estimated seven million homeless people."[172]

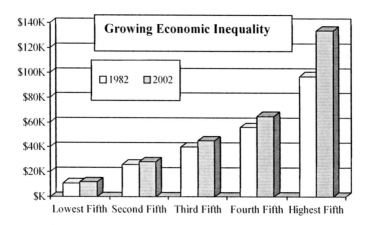

It is not revolutionary to address socio-economic inequality – it is quite conservative. We are trying to conserve our political system by taking care of its citizens. When multi-ga-billionaire dad, Papa Gates is against cutting the estate tax,[173] it makes us

---

[170] *NatYouthSurvey2000*.
[171] At age 11 Amber Coffman founded "Happy Helpers for the Homeless" to feed the poor in Glen Burnie, Maryland. See: heartofamerica.org/speakers/ambercoffman.htm.
[172] *Future500*. Information on homelessness came from the glossary in the front matter.
[173] "One of the oldest and most common forms of taxation is the taxation of property held by an individual at the time of their death. ...An estate tax is a charge upon the decedent's entire estate, regardless of how it is disbursed." See: law.cornell.edu.

wonder what we are giving up. Does renaming it the "death tax" abate the public policy rationale behind the law? What about the double taxing of stock dividends? What does this mean for our retirement? We are not saying that millionaires are evil or that they don't deserve to pass down their riches to their heirs. In fact, we are in favor of tax cuts, but we are just questioning which cuts are most important and what are the consequences of these cuts.

There is a unique ideological breakdown when it comes to Millennials. Of those of us in college, thirty-one percent are conservative on economic issues (versus twenty-five percent economic liberals) and thirty-seven percent are liberal on social issues (versus twenty-five percent socially conservative).[174] We believe in the free market and we refuse to turn our back on social problems.

Educational Marginalization

Economic class is not just about minimum, or living, wage; it is also about access to higher education. To the extent that social class is fluid, education is the key. In the landmark case *Brown v. Board of Education*, the U.S. Supreme Court declared that segregation was unconstitutional as 'inherently unequal.' Analogous to this, "we contend that many of the public schools in the United States are in violation of the Constitution in that they are providing unequal educational opportunities."[175] From the earliest years of our country, universal public education has been critical to the strength of our democracy (and our economy). But access is not enough when some kids are benefiting tremendously from wealthy, strong school systems and others are scraping by with multi-decade old books and not enough classrooms (or even bathrooms) for their students.

---

[174] *CampusKids.*
[175] Behr, Gregg et al. The Content of Our Character, p. 20.

Money is not the panacea to our school's failings, but it would help solve some of the problems created by inequality.

Affirmative Action

As a generation we are divided on affirmative action.[176] This issue took center stage for our generation in the 1990s, especially in states like California where the four decade long program ended.[177] The end of affirmative action profoundly changed schools in California. The higher ranked, but public, University of California, Los Angeles (UCLA) has wealthier students than the lower ranked private, University of Southern California (USC). Both UCLA and USC are great universities, but our point here is how money divides us. Today, wealth influences educational opportunities more than race does. If you can afford to take Kaplan classes, to study with private tutors and to attend better-funded schools in wealthy neighborhoods, then you're more likely to get into the higher ranked college. The savage inequalities of American high schools has a lot more to do with money than it does race – albeit true that these factors are highly correlated.

These changes in affirmative action did not go unquestioned. Millennials at UCLA protested how these changes have affected the ethnic and racial make up of their campus, but these protests were misguided. California does not need to move backwards to 1960s solutions to address this problem. Affirmative action needs a 21st century update.

Texas and Florida also eliminated race considerations from admission, but they instituted a system that guaranteed the top ten percent of all high school graduates could go to college to achieve the compelling interest of a diverse student body. This plan works, but it only works because high schools are so

---

[176] "50% say affirmative action is still needed to counteract discrimination as long as there are no rigid quotas and 44% say affirmative action programs should be phased out because they unfairly discriminate against non-minorities." According to *KFFSurvey*.
[177] Affirmative Action began in 1965 with President Lyndon Baines Johnson.

segregated in those states (and other states). California is beginning to consider "hardship" in their admissions, which acknowledges that a poor student with a 1300 on her SATs might be as smart as a rich kid with a 1350 on her SATs. The much debated Michigan system also considers hardship, but to a much lesser extent than race. These are steps in the right direction, but let's just call it what it is – economic hardship – and give it the weight it deserves. This weight should not be more important than academic record, but not less than racial or ethnic identity.

We may be able to eliminate all types of affirmative action in the future if we can just make high school funding more equal. If we could level the playing field at age fourteen or younger, then we could all fairly compete for the most selective Universities at age eighteen.

Digital Divide

As the Internet revolutionizes society and makes information accessible to all those who have access to a computer, many are left behind. Despite the falling cost of technology and the efforts of the government to make the Internet accessible

> **Youth Activism Resource: Oxfam America**
> Oxfam's Change Initiative encourages young adults to challenge their notions of social justice around the world, especially regarding the issues of poverty and hunger. Oxfam provides resources to young activists to help fight economic injustice.
> www.oxfamamerica.org

in public libraries and schools, a digital divide has evolved between those who can afford the technology and those who cannot. Literacy and access to books used to be the most significant problem in education, but in today's world technological fluency is almost as important as reading, writing and arithmetic.

This divide poses a threat to our future. On a whole, students who attend public school, poor students, and minority (especially African-American) students do not have the same access to technology, as do wealthier, private school students. While over four out of five rich folks have access to the Internet, only about one in five poor people do.[178] Why that fifth rich person is opting out of the Information Revolution, we are not sure, but in today's ultra-digital age, the lack of access for the poor is startling. Government and philanthropic initiatives are working to close this gap by providing computers and Internet connections in schools and libraries, but the divide persists in part due to more constraints on time, fewer computers in homes, and a smaller percentage of parents encouraging them to get on line.

Within the first decade of a new technology, this disparity due to wealth is not surprising. However, it is too important to ignore, especially since it appears that economics is not the only factor. According to Donna L. Hoffman, a professor of management at Vanderbilt University in Nashville, "whites consistently have more Internet access compared with black people with comparable education and incomes."[179] Now that the Internet has become such an important part of our education system, our commercial practices and increasingly our political power, we cannot leave anyone behind.

As new technologies develop, we need to pay attention to emerging divides. For example, if genetic engineering takes off, will the rich have unimaginable advantages over the poor? Or, as health care expenses continue to skyrocket, will our country be divided between those who have health insurance and those who don't? America cannot let this generation grow up as two divided groups; not divided by race, political orientation, or geographic location, but divided by access to advancing technology, health care coverage, or educational opportunity.

---

[178] According to the U.S. Dept of Commerce in 2000, 86.3% of households earning $75,000 and above per year had Internet access compared to 12.7% of households earning less than $15,000 per year. See: digitaldividenetwork.org.

[179] Belluck, Pam. "What Price Will Be Paid." *NYT*, 9/22/99, p. G12.

United Generation

Some of us in the generation are involved in a new union movement very much separate from the current labor establishment and yet not so far from many of the same ideals. We, as a generation, are not individualistic and find power in group organizing and mass movements. The anti-sweatshop movement on college campuses was not a "union" issue, but it was certainly all about labor. It didn't take much for those campus coalitions to then focus on fair wage campaigns and more domestic union issues.

Case Study: Fair Wage Campaign

The longest student sit-in in the 300+ year history of Harvard University was not about Vietnam or apartheid, but rather the minimum wage. During exam periods, in the spring of 2002, twenty-five students staged a twenty-one day sit-in to fight for living wage for University employees.

Boston had passed a fair wage bill a few months earlier, but it did not hold the University accountable since they were in the neighboring city of Cambridge. Despite the fact that Harvard is the wealthiest educational institution in the world, the University was not paying all of their employees a living wage.

So these Millennials protested. They ordered Thai food with their cell phones to be delivered to the President's office. They studied while they fought for social justice, and they won.

They were not alone.

Youth Activist Step #8
Invite the Press on Board

The Harvard students knew that they would only win if the public got upset and Harvard's reputation was put into question. It didn't happen quickly or easily, but ask any of them and they'd say without the press and public on board they would have lost (and failed out of school!).

Presidential candidate Al Gore tried to tap into this with his 2000 campaign theme, "I am for the People not the Powerful." The message came up short in the election, because explicit classism for political ends is not welcome by the young or the old. Especially when political candidates on the left and right have their campaigns financed by the same wealthy and corporate interests. However, the concept (if not the delivery) resonated with many young people on the left in this generation. We are generally skeptical of tax policy and legislation that disproportionately benefits the wealthy and/or the elderly when the poor, middle class and young in this country need so much. We don't want a class war of poor rising up against the rich, but we also don't want a class war of the rich systemically keeping the poor down.

Despite our generation's self-confidence and activism on many levels, on a whole we have become very cynical about poverty and don't see much difference between the political parties. We don't see any national leaders speaking up. We don't hear the media raising their voice. Who will fight for the rights of the poor, the middle class and the young – the vast majority of our country has no one looking out for their interests! Where is our Abraham Lincoln or our Andrew Jackson? Marian Wright Edelman[180] certainly cannot do it alone – it takes a whole village to leave not one child behind.

The United State of America, Inc.

Corporate money in politics may be one reason to explain the inequities in tax policy and government legislation. With the current role of money in political campaigns, it is no surprise that rich CEOs yield so much influence in the political dialogue and are not being held accountable for corporate malfeasance. Even before Enron was front-page news, Millennials have been fighting the increased corporatization of America. In 1999, the Students Transforming and Resisting Corporations (STARC) Alliance was formed to challenge corporate power in pursuit of greater economic equality and truer democracy.

---

[180] Marian Wright Edelman is the founder of the Children's Defense Fund. See childrensdefense.org.

There is a divide among Millennials between "No Logo" activists and brand name consumerist youth. Some of us fight the labor exploitation of the Gap, and others of us gleefully swing dance in our Gap khakis. (Some of us mistakenly do both.) Despite the obvious variance in political ideologies among Millennials, there are some common themes regarding corporations. Most importantly, Millennials are not the same as the communist and socialist youth of previous generations fighting against the capitalist system. The overwhelming majority of young people are capitalist; however, some of them are fighting the evils of capitalist excess, and corporate influences undermining democracy. We want to improve the system, not throw it out. Because Millennials agree on this issue from a common vantage point – capitalism is good – we can look for solutions to some of the system's problems without having to debate the system.

Rich Dad, Poor Kid

Former Presidential candidate Bill Bradley said, "Child poverty is a kind of slow-motion national disaster, and should be treated with the same kind of 'wholesale rescue' the government undertakes after hurricanes."[181] Bradley may not have won the nomination, but he was onto our concerns about financial disparity. And frankly, the most under-appreciated concern our generation has with money is not between the rich and the poor, but the old versus the young. "For over twenty five years, there has been a progressive shift in federal (as well as state and local) spending towards seniors."[182] The worst part is – we are partially to blame! Young people have not been voting, not been paying attention, and not been organized to the extent that seniors are. This is all going to change.

---

[181] "Bradley Offers Youth Poverty Plan." *AP*, 10/21/99
[182] *DivGen*, p. 55.

We are not preaching an oncoming generational war, but we are putting the nation on call. We're not going to take the reverse Robin Hood effect of our generation. We will not let our wealthy elders steal from poorer future generations. Where will our country be in a decade if current policies remain unchecked? An older, wealthier, whiter generation will be counting on a younger, poorer, more diverse generation to take care of them after they ignored us for so many years. For centuries the mantra of good American parenting was, "I want a better life for my kids. I hope they have more opportunity than I had." Today this notion of sacrifice, gratitude delayed, and investment in the future is out the window for far too many aging Boomers.

"The test of the morality of a society is what it does for its children." –
Dietrich Bonhoeffer, German Protestant theologian

9

PUBLIC TRUST

As the sum total of all students in America, there are few issues more relevant to us as a generation than education. However, education is not the only public service that the government has a responsibility to guarantee. We also care deeply about the big-ticket items such as health care and retirement savings. These public obligations command a significant percentage of our national budget, and as we examine current and future policy problems, we realize some changes need to be made to address these very important issues. Unlike our parents or older siblings, we trust the government to do what is right and provide us with these services.[183] We trust, but we still demand better services.

Education

According to William Strauss and Neil Howe, Millennials are "probably the most all-around capable teenage generation this nation, and perhaps the world, has ever seen."[184] Since the early 1970s, high school graduation rates have risen and the number of dropouts has fallen.[185] Starting with the end of

---

[183] "Half [of Millennials] say they trust government to do what's right all or most of the time – twice the share of older people answering the same question in the same poll." *Millennials2College*, p. 9.

[184] *Millennials2College*, p. 77.

[185] *Census*, 12/24/00 Report, P-23, No. 188, p. 2.

Generation X, the number of young Americans attending college has skyrocketed, especially in the last few years. According to the U.S. Department of Labor, a record 67 percent of 1997 high school graduates were enrolled in colleges and universities in the fall of that year. In 1972 that number was less than 50 percent.[186] SAT scores were at a 27-year-high in 2003.[187] With the advent of government programs such as Head Start, even nursery school enrollment has more than doubled since 1973.[188]

Despite our unprecedented amount of schooling, we believe that there are a lot of problems with the education system that must be addressed. At the 2000 National Youth Convention education policy was the focus of much conversation and debate centered on money and youth participation within the schools. The young leaders at this convention took the position that, "Economic disparities should not affect one's quality of, and access to, education," and also that, "Students are marginalized in school systems and there is little significant interaction between teachers, administrators and students. Decisions are made *for* students rather than *with* them."[189]

> **Youth Activism Resource:**
> **The CIRCLE: The Center for Information and Research on Civic Learning and Engagement**
> The CIRCLE promotes research on the civic and political engagement of Americans between the ages of 15 and 25. The CIRCLE is a clearinghouse for relevant information and scholarship. CIRCLE was founded in 2001 with a generous grant from The Pew Charitable Trusts and is based in the University of Maryland's School of Public Affairs.
> www.civicyouth.org

When states rushed to education testing to measure student success, many young activists reacted with alarm. Testing Is Not The Answer is a group of teens at East Chapel Hill High School

---

[186] See: dol.gov and nces.ed.gov.
[187] *Millennials2College*, p. 77.
[188] *Census*, 12/24/02 Report, P-23 No 188, p. 2.
[189] *NYP 2000*, p. 4.

who organize against high stakes testing and raise awareness about education reform issues.[190] Millennials are generally not radicals regarding education reform; we don't believe the entire system needs to be thrown out. However, changes need to be made to allow for federal financial support and creative local initiatives that do not give up on public schools. More support and less rigorous testing are required to create a flexible environment that holds individuals accountable without a one size fits all measure to appraise academic competence.

Patrick Welsh, a high school teacher for twenty-five years in Washington, DC, has a unique perspective on how education has changed over the last quarter-decade. "Over the past two years the test scores of black kids have been rising at a faster rate than those of whites." He does not necessarily attribute this rise to the actions of schools, administrators or teachers, but rather to a noticeable change in student's attitude. "People here don't call guys suckers or sell-outs if they get good grades."[191] Peers play an important role in the motivation (and performance) of the students.

He also says there has been a change in the attitude of parents. "The parents I know who were students of mine in the 70s invariably emphasized education to their kids more than their parents did to them."[192] Ask any teacher and they will tell you that a positive change in attitude among students, their peers, and their parents, is the most important difference in improving the education of young Americans. A positive attitude about education is even more important than wiring every school or hiring 100,000 more teachers.

Not only the attitudes toward learning, but also the methods of teaching are changing. Young people attend charter schools, magnet schools, and private schools with vouchers; and, we are

[190] *Project540*, p. 73.
[191] Welsh, Patrick. "Its No Longer Uncool To Do Well In School." *WashPost*, 3/14/99. p. B01.
[192] Welsh, Patrick. Ibid, p. B01.

generally more supportive of these programs because of the choices they offer.[193] Significantly more families are opting to home school their children.[194] Service learning is growing and hundreds of thousands of Millennials are doing a year of service before pursuing undergraduate or graduate degrees.

Zero Tolerance

Zero tolerance is deficient public policy at best and very harmful at worst. "Since the mid 1990's, every state and the District of Columbia have adopted some form of zero tolerance, to be interpreted by local districts. Some have led to excesses. A 2000 report by the Civil Rights Project at Harvard University and the Advancement Project, a nonprofit legal-assistance group, documented abuses. A six-year-old in Pittsburgh, for example, was suspended last Halloween for carrying a plastic axe as part of a fireman's costume."[195] An eleven-year-old was hauled off in a police van for packing a plastic knife in her lunchbox to cut chicken; a fifth grader was expelled for a year for hiding razor blades from a friend he thought might use them to harm another; and two eight-year-olds were arrested for making terrorist threats and wielding a paper gun in class.[196] In response to such abuses, the American Bar Association passed a resolution in 2002 calling for an end to zero-tolerance policies.[197]

Lee Konetschny, a teacher in Pittsburgh said, "The irony is that students today are easier to teach – better prepared, more considerate of one another, less given to defiance. I don't see

---

[193] According to *KFFSurvey:* "73% of young adults favor giving parents more options through school vouchers."

[194] The rise in home schooling is very recent: "Home schooling was illegal in 30 states in 1980 and has been legal in all states only since 1993." Roduta, Charlie, "The practice of home schooling is on the rise." Ft Wayne News Sentinel, 5/30/03, p. A1. By the spring of 1999 "an estimated 850,000 students nationwide were being homeschooled ... 1.7% of U.S. students." According to *NCES*, see: nces.ed.gov/pubs2001/2001033.pdf.

[195] Leland, John. "Zero Tolerance Policies Change Life at One School." *NYTimes*, 04/08/01, Section 9, p. 1.

[196] Wald, Johanna. "The Failure of Zero Tolerance." *Salon*, 08/29/01.

[197] See: abanet.org.

much gratuitous cruelty."[198] In fact, during the 1990s, while the societal perception of the frequency of student deaths increased, the actual numbers declined.[199]

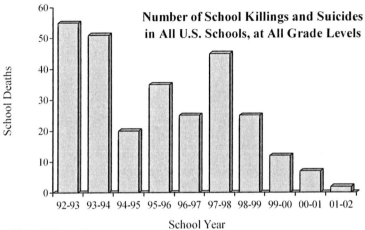

Civic Education

Far too many people in our generation are graduating without a basic civic education – and when civic education does exist in the classrooms, it far too often teaches passivity and disengagement, or limits the intricate beauty of our political system to the basic structure of the government. The paucity of civic education in America has reached such a state of crisis that the powerful service leaders (the Pew Charitable Trust, the Carnegie Corporation of New York, and the Corporation for National Service) all teamed up in 2003 to release a report on how to improve the civic mission of schools. [200] The fact is that most high schools today only require a single course in government – compared to as many as three courses in democracy, civics and government that were common until the 1960s. Recommendations included establishing new civic education curricula, including current events in classroom

---

[198] Leland, John. Ibid, p. 1.
[199] Chart from *Millennials2College*, p. 9. Information in the chart from the National School Safety Center (2002).
[200] See: civicmissionofschools.org.

conversation, and offering extra curricular activities that provide opportunities for students to get involved in the community. Personally, we believe that <u>Millennial Manifesto</u> should be required reading, but we'll settle with teens being able to discuss the newspaper in classrooms.

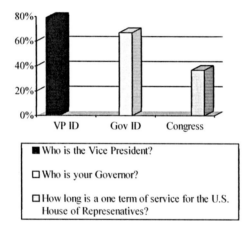

High School Civic Education
Percentage of High School students who can correctly identify the Vice President, their Governor and the length of term of a U.S. House member:

■ Who is the Vice President?

□ Who is your Governor?

□ How long is a one term of service for the U.S. House of Represenatives?

The above graph is a little unfair because it doesn't provide comparative information for adults; however, it is important information. Knowing the basic players in government and broadly how the system works is a prerequisite for being a contributing member of our polis. If you don't know who the baseball players are or understand the game, you're not going to pay attention. Politics should not be as foreign as the sport of cricket to American teens.

Cost of College Education

College enrollment is up, but so too is the cost of those degrees. In 2003, tuition at four-year public institutions went up 14.1 percent according to the College Board. At the same time, Congress has made cuts to the education awards in AmeriCorps and considered reducing support for federal financial aid. Furthermore, with the poor economy and federal tax cuts has caused budget crisis in the states (such as California's budget problems).

Cuts in state funding from the State of Maryland for higher education caused tuition to increase by approximately twenty percent in 2002 and again by 11 percent in 2003. As a result, University of Maryland students responded by creating the Student Citizens Action Network and a Political Action Committee (PAC) with the goal of raising $50,000 in ninety days.[201] Tim Daly, student government president at the University of Maryland College Park is the chairman of this new PAC. Daly said the new PAC "would give students 'a seat at the table' in future budget deliberations. 'This goes beyond just having a sit-in, a protest, a march or a rally.'"[202] As Tim and the students at Maryland are demonstrating, our generation won't sit idly by and watch Congress cut our educational opportunities.

Health Care

The issue of lack of health care is quickly going from bad to worse. "Two million more people are uninsured now than two years ago, and a growing share of those uninsured are young people."[203] Nearly nine out of ten Millennials support efforts to expand health insurance coverage – including 37 percent who

---

[201] PACs give money to elect certain candidates who support certain issues.
[202] Dressler, Michael. "UM students form PAC to protest tuition rise." *The Baltimore Sun*, 10/21/03. See: www.sunspot.net/news/yahoo/bal-md.tuition21oct,0,3211346.story
[203] Weiner, Robert and Amy Rieth. "The Dwindling Youth Vote: Where Will It Be In 2004?" *The Christian Science Monitor*, 06/23/03.

would support a major program that would require a tax increase.[204] Because we are generally young and healthy (although a little obese), the plight of uninsured young adults is going unnoticed by our government. In 2000, one in four of the 50 million Americans without health care were under the age of eighteen.[205] Thirty percent of people 18 to 24 years old were without health insurance for the entire year.[206] Our health care system has not kept pace with our changing economy. Benefits are currently funneled through employers to employees. However, our generation is transient and companies have been cutting back on coverage. We move, change jobs, switch employers and explore new careers. Unlike previous generations of Americans who stuck with one company for a lifetime, we will have an average of seven different careers in our lifetime. Government structures need to be overhauled to keep pace with this new economy.

Ted Halstead of the New America Foundation outlined a system of mandatory self-insurance with a public health insurance safety net for the genuinely needy. This innovative solution is the kind of new idea we need. We don't need to socialize medicine or to sue companies that make fatty foods to solve all of our problems; but rather we need a national program that keeps our nation healthy. And we need a political system that is not so heavily influenced by special interests and money that it allows proposals like mandatory self-insurance to be debated in Congress and not just in DC think tanks.

Health insurance is not the only medical issue facing our generation. While few youth activists are fighting for mandatory self-insurance, thousands of Millennials are fighting to address global AIDS, cancer and even mental health. Especially since the majority of our generation is self-confident and upbeat,

---

[204] According to *KFFSurvey*.
[205] *NYP 2000*, p 8.
[206] *Census*, 12/03

depression and teen suicide often rank among the most important issues facing teens today and these concerns are so often overlooked by older members in our society.[207]

Case Study: The AIDS Treatment Access Initiative
    Alex Bradford helped organized the Student Global AIDS Walk in the spring of 2003. When Alex and other students learned that 8,000 people are dying a day from AIDS, they decided they had to do something.

    The Student Global AIDS Walk, a project of the Student Global AIDS Campaign and the Elizabeth Glaser Pediatric AIDS Foundation, is an initiative that supports programs that treat people with HIV/AIDS in developing countries.

Youth Activist Step #9
Have Your Event
On April 12, 2003, 1,200 people in ten difference cities across the county walked to raise over $80,000 for AIDS. This event was so ambitious that people told them they could never do it. Don't ever let someone tell you what you cannot do.

    The Student Global AIDS Campaign connected nearly 350 high school and college campuses across the country around the critical issue of health care. The stats on this should scare you: "Each year there are 40,000 new HIV infections in the United States, half of which occur in individuals under the age of twenty-five. Every hour, two young people in the United States between the ages of thirteen and twenty-four contract HIV."[208] "One in five HIV infections occurs in people under the age of 25. The HIV epidemic is spreading at the rate of 6,000 new infections each day [worldwide]."[209] SARS may have shut down Hong Kong and Toronto, but AIDS is tearing apart the entire continent of Africa and affecting us heavily here at home. This is not a gay

---

[207] According to a poll done by Do Something and Harris Interactive, 53% listed depression and teen suicide as an important or very important issue to them making it one of the top ten issues of the poll. Viewed on coach.dosomething.org on 12/10/02.
[208] *NNYKit*, p. 2JJDPA.
[209] *NYP 2000*, p. 8.

disease, a black disease, a male disease, or an urban disease. This is a disease that still has no cure and has affected people we know. Those of us with an eye on the future know that this is a global problem that is already spinning out of control.

Retirement

Unlike education and health care, social security is not consistently ranked as a top generational priority. However, this is an issue that we need to watch closely. Boomers may kill Social Security and Gen Xers may be concerned they are not going to get it, but our generation is the *least* likely to see Social Security cover our retirement expenses. So listen up! Don't skip this section, because it has important information about our generation.

Social Security used to be the third rail in American politics – just how touching the third rail of the subway system will end your life, touching social security could end your political career. With political courage, George W. Bush changed that in 2000 when he made a calculated appeal to reach out to Gen X and propose innovative market-based approaches to address the problem.

Few Millennials are organizing WTO-style protests of the Social Security Administration's policies; however, some Gen X activists have taken the lead on this. Organizations like the 2030 Center and Third Millennium have fought to educate youth about the future of retirement and possible alternatives to current Social Security policy. Some conservatives move toward privatization to increase the rate of return, while liberals argue against privatization because of the increased exposure to risk. Quite frankly, we've found very few young people who care about the specifics of this issue as long as there is money in the program at the end of the day. Whether that will be the case remains to be seen, but one thing is for certain: if we don't look after our own future we will have no one to blame but ourselves if we retire financially in the red. We sure would like the government to be there for us, but we'll open our own 401(k)s while we wait for the government to clean up its mess. The stock market may be up or down in the short-term, but we have confidence that in forty years when we want to retire, the money from the private sector will be there for us. However, not all of us can afford 401(k)s and for those of us who need it the most, we are counting on the government to make sure social security is available.

Taxes

This chapter would be incomplete without taking a quick look at taxes. Certainly none of these social programs can be paid for without taxes. While some of us are too young to be paying a great deal of taxes, we all know that down the road we'll be stuck paying our fair share. As a neo-fiscal conservative generation, we do not want a large government and we do favor a balanced budget. We want fewer taxes, but not at the expense of social programs. According to a Harvard University study of college students, "Fifty-one percent [of college students] support a cut in the federal income tax, but only eighteen percent support an income tax cut if it would result in a 'reduction in social programs such as healthcare, education or welfare.'"[210] For many young conservatives this is the most important issue our country is facing, but for most of us we just want a government that works, is not taking more than it needs, and is spending wisely whatever it is taking. Oh, and by the way, we'd like to make sure that since we do pay taxes, we at least get something back in the form of government programs.[211] Don't cut taxes for the rich (and often older generations) and then cut social programs, like AmeriCorps, which fight poverty and involve the participation of our generation.

---

[210] *CampusKids*, p. 6.
[211] Teens pay an estimated $9.7 billion in sales tax. See: youthrights.org/vote10.html#4.

PART THREE:

TODAY AND BEYOND

"Whether you're a citizen, student or activist, a voter or a non-voter, one thing is clear: democracy in the US is not living up to its name. Just over a year after the 2000 elections memorable for butterfly ballots, voter intimidation, illegal voter roll purges, and the Supreme Court "selection" of the President, young people are still being told that we're apathetic because we don't participate! In a democracy full of corruption, racism, monotony and inequality, our question is, "Participate in what!?" – **Democracy Action Project**

10

YOUTH VOTE

When looking at the political future of the generation, we should start with the recent history – especially the campaign and election of 2000 (E2K) and what these years mean for our generation's future. The election controversy, particularly the hundreds of thousands of uncounted votes nationally, made the country cry out for reform. In Florida, the House and Senate passed a bill that sets statewide standards for elections, ushering in optical scanning ballot systems in time for 2002 elections and doing away with hanging chads and butterfly ballots. A few years later the Help America Vote Act (HAVA) passed to take election reform a step beyond just updating machines from the 1920s.

While Palm Beach County dominated the news, there remains the untold story of Millennials running for office, young people calling for reform, and the youth reaction to the historic event. The 2000 Election was an exciting time period that clearly affected the way Millennials think and behave. As Millennial Andrea Perullo put it, "I think the closeness of the election definitely turned people on. How could it not? It was in your face everywhere you went." Heather Moore was a student at James Madison University. She said there was commotion in the halls as Florida kept changing colors on the television. Heather felt "that the age old saying 'My vote doesn't matter' just got thrown out."[212]

Millennials even invented a new way to end run the 200+-year-old Electoral College. With an innovative, web-based system called "Nader Trader," Nader supporters in battleground states traded their votes for Gore votes in states that were blowouts. Since almost every state has a winner-take-all system in the Presidential election, then if you don't live in a battleground state your vote has a lower chance of actually making a difference in the final outcome. Therefore creative voting-age Millennials said buzz off to the Electoral College by trading votes online in an effort to try to elect Gore and also find Nader his five percent to create a strong national party. Wouldn't election reform be easier?

With less than half the country voting in non-presidential year congressional elections, we must question the health of democracy. The system needs to be changed for young and old Americans. Further, because of low overall turnout, the opportunities for Millennials to rock the system through voting are huge.

Third Parties

We, as Millennials, continue some of the Gen X trends to adhere less to party alignment than Boomers by registering as Independent and engaging in split ticket voting. This is due, in part, because of what we have learned from the political landscape. A twelve-year-old Gen Xer, born in 1968, would have witnessed John Anderson, a major third party candidate for President in 1980, receive about six percent of the votes. A ten-

---

[212] Andrea Perullo and Heather Moore's quotes come from emails to Scott Beale.

year-old Millennial, born in 1982, would have witnessed Ross Perot receive almost twenty percent of the votes with a realistic chance of actually winning. Furthermore, that same Millennial was sixteen when pro-wrestling sensation Jesse Ventura became the second Governor in the 90s elected on a third party ticket. Our generation's willingness to vote third party has been shaped by many factors, including: the decline of the strength of political parties, the increase in the role of media in elections, the increased focus on personality in elections, and the above mentioned Xer willingness to vote third party out of desperation and disgust with the system.

However, we have not given up on the political parties like so many Gen Xers have. "A Close Up Foundation survey of 500 high school students learned that Millennials share a rather traditional view of political parties – which they consider useful, albeit too argumentative."[213] We are not blindly loyal to parties that have ignored us or too blind to see that third parties rarely work. As a generation, we are far too practical to vote for third parties en masse, unless we are successful in our fight for election reform.

Election Reform

Instant run off voting (IRV) is an idea whose time has come, but the parties fear it and the public is not yet unaware of it. IRV is a system that lets you rank your candidates and guarantees that the winner of the election earns a majority of the vote. For example, a voter in Florida might rank his top three choices as Pat Buchanan, George Bush, Al Gore, then Ralph Nader. When the polls closed, if no candidate won a majority of the first choice votes, then the computer would eliminate the candidates who received the least amount of votes. Eventually you would have two candidates remaining and a winner who earned a

---

[213] Howe and Strauss, <u>Millennials Rising</u>, p. 232.

majority of the votes; in this example our hypothetical voter would have his vote go to George W. Bush.[214]

If IRV legislation were to pass, then it would enable people to vote guilt-free for third or fourth party candidates and also protect the major parties from losing an election to a party that does not command a majority of the population's support. It is revolutionary because it would guarantee a majority vote for the victor without the expense and negative effects of a runoff election. To win, it would be more difficult to appeal to a small set of "base" votes and win over their support; you'd actually have to get people to consider you as their second pick, too. This could also lead to cleaner campaigns since candidates would need to appeal to a broader base. IRV is particularly useful in primary elections when you have multiple candidates. The 2003 MoveOn.org web primary for the Democratic Party resulted in no clear winner of the nine candidates, despite the fact that Dean received almost 44 percent of the vote, nearly doubling the second place finisher.[215] If MoveOn had used IRV, which would have been especially easy online, then the organization could endorse a candidate who commanded a majority of the voters support.

> **Youth Activism Resource: Youth Vote Coalition**
>
> The Youth Vote Coalition is a national, nonpartisan, diverse coalition of organizations established to increase civic participation and political activity among youth. If you want support with your voting efforts, start here.
>
> www.youthvote.org

The technology is available to make such voting possible and easy. It is currently being used in San Francisco, as well as in other cities and countries all over the world. Most importantly, it is being done in dozens and soon hundreds of college student government elections all over the country. By the time Millennials start running for President, IRV will be used

---

[214] For more information on IRV see fairvote.org.

[215] See moveon.org/primary/report.html. Vied on: 06/27/03.

in elections. With our increasingly diverse society, we will need to use a method that guarantees an election winner supported by a majority of the voters.

Voter Turnout

While there are a number of proposals out there to increase voter turnout, there are also many people who argue that we don't need greater turnout. Their argument is that it is better to have well informed voters than simply more voters. This is all well and good, but why can't we have both!?

The government should actively look at ways to promote voting. For example, elections could be held on a Saturday, or over a two-day period. Polls could be open longer. Youth could be recruited to be poll workers to help teach the basics of democracy to our generation. The average age of poll workers in Palm Beach County, Florida is 72-years-old;[216] nationally it is 68-years-old.[217] This is over three times the age of your first time eighteen-year-old voter! Recent election law is beginning to address the poll worker problem, but we can bridge this gap if we take the initiative.

Online Voting

Online voting could revolutionize participation. Imagine this scenario: during lunch, you check out espn.com to see how your fantasy football team is doing, pay your cell phone bill online, and still have time to go vote, too. Online voting would increase the information voters have access to. With access to candidates' bios, incumbent voting records, and party platform information easily available at the time of voting, there would be no excuses for not making an educated vote. It sure would make absentee voting easier, too. Some people are concerned about

---

[216] Minor, Emily. "I Expected Drama As a Poll Worker." *Palm Beach Post*, 3/13/02, p. 10A.
[217] This is the age that is repeatedly cited in "Help America Vote Act" conversations, Youth Vote Meetings, NASS Meetings, and other conversations about poll workers.

the costs of this system, the ramifications of the digital divide, voter intimidation, and the authenticity of each vote. But the technology is there to do this and to make it legitimate.

In 2000, Youth E-Vote sponsored an online election with students from kindergarten to twelfth grade. Fifty-six percent of over one million registered students voted for George W. Bush to become their President. The experience was a very positive one for the Millennials involved. "If you think about it, all of us will be casting votes over the Internet someday -- we may as well begin now!" noted Bryant Hall, a participating high school junior from Galesville, Maryland.[218]

Already, the Net is educating the public a great deal. Project Vote Smart is an outstanding, non-partisan organization located in Montana. They are using web pages (vote-smart.org) and 1-800 numbers to provide non-partisan candidate information. The League of Women Voters has a great site with similar content as well. Dnet.org tells you all about the candidates who will be on your ballot on Election Day. Sadly, many politicians and professional political advisors are fighting against these online systems. Project Vote Smart gives candidates an opportunity to say where they stand on a wide variety of issues, but candidates fear that their opponents will use this information against them. If say-nothing television commercials have replaced meaningful efforts to take stands on issues, then it is long past time for reform. If candidates are working to keep you ill informed, then we have to rise up and demand a better system!

Millennials may one day support many creative types of reform. What about providing a financial incentive to vote? The government shows that it is important for people to save for retirement or to own a home by providing tax credits; what about a $100 tax credit if you vote? What about requiring voting? You would not be forced to choose a candidate, since the ballot

---

[218] 11/2/02 Election.com press release election.com/us/pressroom/pr2000/1102b.htm

could have a "no vote" option. That way we could tell if, in fact, all those people not voting are actually registering their discontent, or just couldn't make it to the polls. How about requiring a half-day off from work, if we insist on doing this thing on a Tuesday. We take time off for parades on the Fourth of July and President's Day, but we cannot have a national half-day off work and school to actually vote for the President? The current two hours doesn't provide enough of a break.

Case Study: Lowing the Voting Age in Cambridge
   Jesse Baer and Paul Heintz were two sixteen-year-old activists with the Campaign for a Democratic Future who led an effort to lower the voting age to sixteen in Cambridge, Massachusetts for municipal elections. They were unsuccessful their first year trying, so they came back the next year, compromised on the age and were successful in lowering the voting age to seventeen. Cambridge became the first city in the country to do this.

**Youth Activism Step #10
Maintain Momentum**
   Everything in life worth having is worth fighting for. Never assume it will be easy and never give up. "We've worked as hard as we can," said Paul Hentz, "'The moral of this story is to keep at it."

   Youth-run organizations like the National Youth Rights Association (NYRA) and Generation Net have been advocating lowering the voting age. In Alaska, Arizona, Florida, Maine, Maryland, Massachusetts, North Dakota, and Texas, bills have been introduced in the state legislature or in city councils to lower the voting age. In Germany legislation has been offered to eliminate the voting age. In England, the Mayor of London has publicly supported lowering the voting age to sixteen. If sixteen-year-olds were allowed to vote, not only would it have the esoteric benefits of expanding democracy in our country and encouraging politicians to pay attention to youth issues, but it would also have the practical benefit of teaching high school students how to vote by voting in their schools.[219] And don't make the mistake of thinking that all of us pimply-faced teens will be Democrats. (Remember: 41%I, 29%D, 26%R)[220] We're most likely to vote with our parents. Or we may even have independent opinions!

Same Day Voter Registration

How about same day voter registration? It is no coincidence that the two states with the highest voter turnout (Maine and Minnesota) also have same day voter registration. In fact, this is an important issue for Millennials because while same day registration increases turnout among all ages, it increases turnout even more for younger voters.

Jason Stefany, the Membership Director of the Wisconsin Democratic Party believes that same day voter registration has made it far easier to increase voting numbers among students. Through "knock and drag" efforts (i.e., knocking on doors and dragging students to the polls), youth voting has been remarkably high in that state. At the University of Wisconsin at Madison, for example, the voter turnout rate was 85 percent for students in the 2000 election, the highest student turnout in the nation.[221]

Could the lack of same day voter registration be more evidence that the parties don't want to hear what we have to say? Are we that unpredictable, that dangerous? We are not unpredictable voters! Don't look at how many of our peers are registered independent or how uncertain their turnout may appear to be. Millennials vote on issues over personality and personality over party.[222] In many cases, the issues we value

---

[219] NYRA has a lot of research on this issue and a great list of reasons to lower the voting age, see: youthrights.org/vote10.html

[220] *CampusKids*

[221] Burd, David. "Civic Engagement with Political Engagement." University of Pennsylvania, JWS Senior Research Paper. 05/02/02, p. 27.

[222] *TrustMatters*, p. 36.

may align with a certain party – young women who are pro-choice tend to vote Democrat. Not because the candidates are Democrats, per se, but because they agree on a certain issue, or set of issues. However, that same nineteen-year-old woman may vote for a different party if a pro-choice Republican comes along who supports education reform that she favors. Issues trump party for Millennials.

We are not dangerous voters; in fact, we are very sensible voters. "Millennials are highly adaptable and have an upbeat, albeit pragmatic outlook on life."[223] Fundamentally, our generation is willing to advocate for change from within the system. When an opportunity arises to vote for a candidate (or a proposition) that supports change that we want, then we will turnout, often in great numbers, to make that change.

The ballot initiative and referendum processes are a good example of this. In general, ballot initiatives can increase turnout in an election by seven to nine percent in a non-presidential election year and three to four and half percent during presidential election years.[224] Ballot initiatives allow the citizens to address issues that legislators are too scared to touch. The whole process, from gathering signatures to public education campaigns, has a very positive effect on turnout. However, ballot initiatives are not shielded from other problems within the system, specifically the role of money. Wealthy people can almost buy new laws with expensive, confusing campaigns and few limits on spending.

In Nevada, election officials saw an increase in the number of eighteen- to twenty-five-year-olds registering to vote when marijuana, abortion and the environment were on the ballot. Eighteen-year-old Eric Renninger said that the proposition motivated him to register to vote. "I wanted to have a say in that

---

[223] Becker, T.J. *ChiTrib*, 1/31/99 "Enter, the Millennials." p. C1.
[224] Tolbert, Gummel and Smith, "The Effect of Ballot Initiatives on Voter Turnout in the American States." American Politics Research, 11/01.

because I don't think government should tell you what to do," he said.[225] One student from Maine said she chose to vote solely on local referendums and initiatives. She stated, "There were state-wide issues that were very important; there was an abortion question, there was a medical marijuana question, and there was another one about allocating a large sum of money for conservation issues."[226] These issues motivated her to vote.

Issues that we care about motivate our generation when we believe our vote can make a difference. We believe that national ballot initiatives should be started to further expand democracy in our country – especially if the effect of big money in campaigns can be controlled.

Why Youth Don't Vote

There are three main reasons why young people do not vote. They do not have enough information, they feel as if their votes may not make a difference, and they are simply not asked to turn out on Election Day. This isn't rocket science. The generation is generally neither stupid nor apathetic. We just feel ignored and powerless.

The E2K taught us all a lot about politics. One thing that it reinforced among young voters is the effect of the Electoral College on voter turnout. A Millennial from Texas may decide that it is not worth the effort to vote in the Presidential election since then-Governor Bush was sure to win his own conservative state. If there was neither a close Congressional election nor a local election with candidates paying attention to her, then she might decide to sit this one out. Groups like the Center for Voting and Democracy are fighting for proportional representation to fix this problem. If a state like California had proportional representation then if 49 percent of the state voted

---

[225] "Young Voters Have Say in Nevada Ballot Initiative" 9/26/02 See:
jointogether.org/sa/news/summaries/reader/0,1854,554504,00.html. Viewed on 4/1/03.
[226] *NewStudentPolitics*, p. ii.

for George W. Bush in the next Presidential Election, then the parties would nearly split the 56 electors, rather than have it go to only one party. Then Republicans in California and Democrats in Texas would no longer feel disenfranchised in a winner-take-all-system.

Our generation is also unmotivated when the election appears to be a landslide. When polling numbers indicate a significant lead for one candidate, we may stay home. We are a generation that has grown up on polling numbers. We understand how they work; we believe in their accuracy. While polls do not guarantee a candidate winning, there are plenty of times when elections are seemingly decided well before Election Day.

Charlie Cook, publisher of a widely respected political newsletter, stated before the 2002 congressional elections, "Not more than two to three dozen of the 435 congressional races will be competitive." The lack of competition is mostly due to money and politics and this was during a time when both the congressional houses and the general public were very evenly divided. After 9-11 and E2K, the 2002 elections had the potential to be an important event across the country, but most incumbents walked to reelection. In fact, over the 210-year history of the congressional races, incumbents have won 85 percent of the time.[227] In our lifetime they have won over 92 percent of the time. For these reasons, many in our generation may not vote unless there are other reasons they are going to the polls.

A few reasons that Millennials may vote include propositions they support (or actively don't support), viable third party candidates, young candidates, or candidates who focus on issues that they care about. We are not a generation of

---

[227] This chart came from: bettercampaigns.org/standard/display.php?StoryID=5.

dangerous or unpredictable voters. We are quite the opposite. If you speak to us, then chances are, we'll speak for you.

Incumbent Re-Election Rates

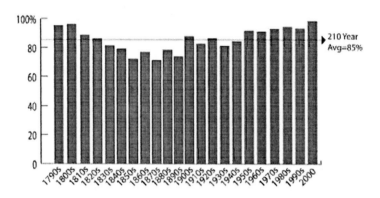

Sources: Vital Statistics on Congress; Congressional Research Service

Money and Politics

It comes down to this: if you don't have the dough, then you don't have the same access to elected officials as those who do. Contrary to popular belief there is not a direct quid pro quo among big money interest and politicians. It is, however, a much more insidious relationship. Candidates and politicians (who are automatically candidates again if they want to run for re-election) are spending far too much time raising money for office when on the campaign trail and raising money again when in office. Public policy decisions do consider political ramifications and in particular how policies may affect donors. Rarely will a big oil tycoon give money to an elected official and tell her how to vote; it is just understood. So, unless you are an independently wealthy candidate, you cannot even try to take the high ground with the money and politics issue. This situation prevents the vast majority of average Americans from running for office.

The other problem with money and politics is how non-representative it is of the general public. In fact, it is not even representative of the wealthy public. "Less than one percent of the population contributes more than 80 percent of all money in federal elections in amounts of $200 or more."[228] We believe that meaningful campaign finance laws need to be enacted, but we can also begin to fix the system by making small donations to candidates that we support. It clearly does not have the same value, but candidates would notice if hundreds of young people contributed to their campaigns and may even pay closer attention to youth issues as a result. Candidate Howard Dean is quite proud of the fact that his average contribution is under $100, and this entirely due to youth participation.

There are a lot of good groups addressing campaign finance reform including Public Campaign, Democracy Matters, Common Cause and the youth-run GenerationNet.org. While many Millennials feel this is very important, we believe that many more have not yet identified campaign finance reform as the solution to the larger problem of feeling disenfranchised. The fact of the matter is that speech in America, especially political speech on television, is not free; but it should be. The Supreme Court and the political parties will continue to debate this issue and play loophole games with campaign fundraising until we take notice of how insidious the current financing of campaigns is to our democracy. And, at the end of the day, while money corrupts our political system, it does not completely take away the power of the vote.

The Low Down

We've interviewed dozens of people working for professional campaigns and the dirty secret in Washington is that candidates do not actually want you to vote! They actively work

---

[228] Bonifaz, John C. "Not the Rich, More Than the Poor." Poverty & Race Research Action Council. Oct.1999. See: prrac.org/topics/sep99/bonifaz.htm Viewed on 06/10/03

to lower voter turnout to a predictable and winnable size. Negative campaigns work by keeping swing voters home and mobilizing the party base supporters against an opponent they demonize. Candidates don't discuss issues because issues are complicated, but emotional appeals to an identified group of voters work well. Political parties only fight over twenty House seats to see who controls Congress and state legislators gerrymander[229] districts to protect incumbents and parties. Election reform that starts with good intentions becomes watered down and the only legislation that can ever pass is for show. It seems impossible to find a majority of elected officials willing to sincerely fix campaign finance, free airtime, or voter representation.

If our generation can bridge the activist gap and the service gap and express our political opinions by voting and not just volunteering or protesting, then Millennials will have a powerful influence over other generations. Although it is a common misconception that Boomers hold a lock over political issues due to their size, Millennials are a larger segment of the population than Boomers are now. Furthermore, we are even a larger generation than the Boomers were twenty years ago when they were our age.

So, in short, the system is messed up; but we are not powerless because of faults in the system. We are powerless because we have chosen not to seize power. If you think we can continue to blame all the problems of the world on our parents, well fugettaboutit, we need to stand up and be heard. We need to be citizens, not spectators.[230] It is time to get off the sidelines.

---

[229] "Gerrymandering" means to draw the boundaries of an electoral district around certain population (e.g. black voters, republican voters.)
[230] This is the motto of the Arsalyn Foundation. For more information on Arsalyn and their civic work see: arsalyn.org.

"Americans must learn once again to rely on themselves for their own defense. Our way of life — our very freedoms — depend on it." –
Thomas Ridge, Director of Homeland Security

11

SEPTEMBER 11, 2001

As kids we were told our generation "had no Vietnam" or any event like Kennedy's assassination: one where we all knew exactly where we were when it happened. If Columbine didn't quiet the skeptics, 9-11 sure did. Not only do all of us know where we were when the planes flew into the World Trade Center, but many of us also witnessed the second plane in person or live on television. This was even more life changing than Kennedy's assassination. This was our generation's Pearl Harbor or bombing of Fort Sumter.[231] This was the Fourth Turning[232] in American history that changed everything.

Our generation joined the nation as we mourned the loss of so many lives. We will forever have the images of victims jumping from the World Trade Center towers to their deaths. As kids, we witnessed the courage of everyday heroes like the New York City Fire Department and civilians on a plane in Pennsylvania. Our generation held on tight as American fighter jets protected our cities. We feared further terrorism and within months were frightened that our mail would deliver unexpected

---

[231] The bombing of Fort Sumter started the Civil War and the bombing of Pearl Harbor started America's involvement in World War II. These events were the second and third turning in American History according to Strauss and Howe.
[232] See information on the Fourth Turning at the back of the book.

evil. Millennials interning in Congress experienced a new kind of politics when the U.S. Senate Offices were moved to safe houses, security was significantly tightened and work remained quite serious long after the fires at the Pentagon were put out.

These were not the only threats we faced. Arab Americans and many non-Arab, dark skinned Americans faced issues of discrimination, racial profiling and violence. Legal immigrants and the most diverse generation in American history were finding civil liberties threatened by a government that wanted to attack terrorism no matter what the cost.

Rally Behind the Flag

Immediately following September 11th, our patriotism soared, our support for the government certainly increased,[233] and we looked to volunteer in any way we could. Like many older Americans, Millennials signed up to donate blood on 9-11. When Millennial Avidan Ackerson was told he was too young to donate blood he decided to try to change the law. A junior in high school at the time, Avidan organized a coalition and coauthored successful state legislation that now allows sixteen-year-olds to donate blood.[234]

Many Millennials signed up for the military the week following September 11th. A number of Millennials rushed into careers in the CIA, FBI, Foreign Service and the military. Applications for many of these branches of the government doubled as Millennials looked for careers that meant something in the public sector. At twenty-three, Courtney Kramer was one of the Millennials who entered the Foreign Service as a Public Diplomacy Officer. This young woman from Missouri wanted to promote America overseas and to change our country's negative reputation abroad. We interviewed another Millennial

---

[233] According to the *CIRCLE*, "69% of youth said the events of 9-11 make them more favorable towards the government."

[234] See: my-redcross.org/html/BloodDriveSchedule.asp last viewed on 06/02/03.

in Los Angeles who signed up for the military immediately following September 11th. An Arab American youth, he wanted to be a soldier in this war to end terrorism.

Although some Millennials flocked toward the military, others began to fly away. The Central Committee for Conscientious Objectors observed that calls to their hotline skyrocketed after 9-11. Students were concerned about the draft, parents wanted to protect their sons, and soldiers currently in the military wanted to find out what their options were. It was time to show your cards; we were entering a new world.

While Congress and the mainstream media feared whispering a word of dissent, many Millennials proclaimed their concern about an ever-spreading war. Even in New York City, some youth activists made their fears of an over-zealous American-military-war-machine just days after the towers fell.

The terrorist events reinvigorated many people within our generation. As students in St. Louis told us, "September 11th makes it hard to be apathetic any more."[235] On the left and the right, we were ready to make sacrifices and to fight for what we believed in, but we were told to shop not save, and buy cars not war

> **Youth Activism Resource:**
> **YouthNOISE**
>
> YouthNOISE is a group of young people--from all 50 states, the District of Columbia and more than 118 countries – together with a group of adults working to provide information from more than 300 nonprofit partners that will spark youth action and voice. YouthNOISE is an initiative of Save the Children Federation, Inc.
> www.youthnoise.com

bonds. This was the first time in our country's history that citizens received a tax cut while at war. There wasn't even a call to service – military, public or community. We were confused, sad and unsure what to do in a poor economy and an uncertain world.

---

[235] Cohen, Yani. Interview with Scott Beale at Washington University on 09/24/01.

Immediately following 9-11 we watched the television to learn more about terrorism, but soon our interest in the news appeared to decline. As a generation we continue to register lower levels of news consumption than previous generations did at a comparable stage in the life cycle.[236] However, many of us are not reading the daily paper and looking to alternative sources of news (i.e. blogs,[237] late night television, or hip hop). According to Harris Interactive, "The percentage of people using the Internet as one of their information sources, if not their primary source, jumped from 64 percent to 80 percent in the two weeks following the attacks, overtaking radio (72%) and second only to television (98%)."[238] This is certainly even higher for Millennials, since we don't identify as closely with the traditional media.

Freedom's Answer

Perhaps it shouldn't be a surprise, but the pollsters, most of the media and much of the public did miss the most incredible generational reaction to September 11th. Early in 2002, a group of young leaders from a wide variety of national youth organizations, decided to come together and rally behind a common goal – to set a record turnout level for the 2002 elections. Although too young to vote, what started with five dynamic leaders turned into twelve key organizers, became 200 lead activists and over swept 2,500 schools across the country. These self-proclaimed members of the "September 11 Generation" named their movement "Freedom's Answer" and set out to shock the world and re-inspire a generation and a nation to civic engagement.

---

[236] *CIRCLE.* "Public's News Habits Little Changed by September 11" 06/06/02.
[237] A "blog" is short for a "web log." It is an online diary where readers can regularly come back for new information.
[238] Nigel Parry, "The Internet as an Alternative News Publishing Medium." *The Electronic Intifada,* 02/27/03. See: electronicintifada.net/v2/article1204.shtml

This group of Millennials was successful; in 2002, the United States saw record turnout for a non-presidential election year with approximately 78.7 million people voting.[239] This was a result of a number of factors, but Freedom's Answer was undoubtedly one of them. Tens of thousands of students pounded the pavement asking people to pledge to vote in honor of those lost on 9-11. "High Tech, High Touch" was their mantra that wed the proven tactic of peer-to-peer (or in this case, youth-to-adult) non-partisan outreach together with all of the tools that the Information Revolution provided for our generation. The website and weekly conference calls with over 200 young leaders allowed these teens to coordinate the largest-ever youth-led get out the vote drive. These students started the year as youth heads of major organizations, but ultimately their "organizational pride turned into generational pride."[240]

It is not, as some would lead us to believe, that young people turned from apathetic to activist in one day. Many of us were already involved, already engaged. However, 9-11 created an historic opportunity for collaboration and motivation. Groups worked together like never before and activists leveraged the opportunity to inspire some who were not yet involved.

Hawks vs. Doves

As the war moved from New York City to Afghanistan to the halls of the United Nations and then Baghdad, our generation grew more concerned each day. We continue to worry about whether we are at Code Yellow, Orange Plus or Fuchsia. We worry about whether more weapons will be found, if more acts of terrorism will occur and how long this reign of terror will last. We want the international community to be involved, but get disturbed when French economic interests seem to be oiling the waters of international negotiations. We are equally upset when

---

[239] Navratil, Wendy. "She's a Winner With Her Red Corvette." *ChiTrib*, 12/01/02, p. Q4.
[240] Clayton, Zach, et. al. <u>Freedom's Answer</u>, p.145.

aggressive U.S. leaders charge full steam ahead without considering the importance of diplomacy, humility or timing.

We are concerned that the Democrats in Congress fell in line right behind the war drum, and the American media establishment embraced the hot new reality show sequel called the "War in Iraq." The media became completely embedded with the soldiers. CNN was not alone. Many networks gave non-stop coverage to the war. Shock and awe for the American viewing public provided hours of nonstop news.

Corporate Media and The War

Just before the war, Comcast Cable made the uncommon decision to reject a political ad that was anti-war. Comcast claims that it held the ad because it could not verify the statements made in it, but it is not a reach to suggest that this cable monolith was trying to curry favor from the Administration. Comcast (now merged with AT&T) owns 70 percent of the top twenty markets. The FCC recently approved regulation that further reduces  competition and Congress is also considering a proposal that would reign in skyrocketing monthly subscriber fees. [241]

Some of us feel Clear Channel is just as politically motivated. This radio giant, who owns 1,233 radio stations across the country, organized rock concerts in favor of the war.[242] These pep rallies / indirect lobbying events did not appear to tap into the youth attitude towards the war, but rather tried to influence young people to support the Administration's point of view. Many activists were concerned since Clear

---

[241] Graphic: Project YANO permission from Rick Jahnkow

[242] Jones, Tim. "Media Giant's Rally Sponsorship Raises Questions." *ChiTrib*, 3/19/03, p. C6.

Channel's Vice Chairman is a big financial supporter of President Bush[243] and certainly wants FCC Chairman Michael Powell (son of Secretary of State Colin Powell) on his side. Ten years ago Clear Channel owned 43 stations, but deregulation of the government allowed this radio monopolist to multiply. Bush told the world that you are either with us or against us, and Comcast and Clear Channel know which side they are on.

War(s) Overseas

Peace loving Millennials may have gotten most of the press, but there is no anti-war consensus among youth. Millennial CNN reporters like Jason Bellini brought the war into our homes and we paid attention as soldiers our age fought and died overseas. Millennials were the heroes and the soldiers who fought this war. Female pilots, cooks and mechanics showed the diversity and strength of our generation. Despite what you may see in Army commercials, we showed the military really did have more than one person on their team.[244]

Millennials will not give the government a blank check to fight the Axis of Evil overseas, but it has been granted a very long leash. Terrorism must be addressed, diplomacy must be used and evil must be met. We're proud to be Americans and to have our country and our military play a leading role in shaping the world, but the international community is not served by an overzealous nation taking unilateral action inadvertently creating resentment toward America in an effort to wipe out evil. As C.S. Lewis taught us, "War creates no absolutely new situation: it simply aggravates the permanent human situation so that we can no longer ignore it."[245]

---

[243] "Clear Channel Executive Denies Pro-War Rallies Were Ordered." *San Diego Union-Tribune*, 03/31/03 p. D6.
[244] It is our personal belief that the Army "An Army of One" slogan does not resonate with Millennials. We're team oriented and the last thing we want to do is fight alone.
[245] See: quotes.telemanage.ca/quotes.nsf/quotes/93b77b541751b26b85256cdb000fb72b.

Peace Activists

While some Millennial women served in the military, others served the country by protesting military action. Millennial activist Maritza Valenzuela joined forces with Boomer women to question the government's war machine with a group called "Code Pink." Gabriella Smith is a ten-year-old member of Code Pink. This fifth grader organized the Takoma Park Kids for Peace. "I'm half-Palestinian, and I don't want another war in the Middle East,"[246] she told reporters from the Washington Post.

Case Study: Teen Web Online

Billy Hallowell created Teen Web Online as a response to the Columbine shootings. His works with Teen Web has landed him on shows such as NBC's The John Walsh Show and national magazines. Through the website Billy works on issues such as sex, violence, discrimination, personal image and drug use. In addition to doing work addressing Columbine and these current issues, Billy and his site are trying to further peace in local communities and around the world.

In response to the war in Iraq, Billy said that he supported the President and it "is essential that teenagers and adults alike work to stop the violence in our own communities."

Youth Activist Step #11: Develop a Community of Support

Billy knows that is important that you surround yourself with other young activists who can keep you going and help you avoid burnout. Anyone can be a youth activist for a summer, or two years, but do you have the stamina to keep it up? This is different than building a coalition to support a project; this is building a community to keep you going over time.

Across the country from Walter Johnson High School near Washington, DC to Lowell High School in San Francisco, hundreds of students walked out of classrooms to protest the war

---

[246] Moreno, Sylvia and Lena H. Sun. "In Effort to Keep the Peace, Protesters Declare 'Code Pink'." *WashPost*, 03/09/03 p. C01.

in Iraq. Teachers and students alike were surprised by the turnout at these walkouts. If you listened to the media, it seemed that everyone in the country was behind the war, and besides, young people don't care anyhow. The Lowell High student paper reported, "Students' willingness to walk out of class — risking unexcused absences, zeros on tests, police action and other unforeseen consequences — definitely left an imprint."[247]

All over the country our generation was protesting the war. "On March 5th, 2003, on the eve of the war with Iraq, almost 500 high school and college campuses participated in the 'Books Not Bombs' student strike to tell politicians and school administrators that we were against a war with Iraq."[248] Students were concerned about the cost of the war (and cuts in education), so they launched a "Books Not Bombs" national student lobby day. The activists connected politics to their activism by registering students to vote and taking their complaints to Congress and the White House. Some politicians compared these protests and walkouts to mere focus groups,[249] but for these kids the feeling of solidarity was a refreshing change from feeling isolated with unpopular views.

The Long Haul

While Boomer leaders were unable to have a meaningful conversation with France, Millennial youth were opening up dialogue with Iraqi youth. Funded in part 'by the Shei'rah Foundation and NHK of Japan, and produced by the Downtown Community Television Center and NextNext Entertainment, this live satellite conversation allowed American and Iraqi youths the

---

[247] "Walkout Gives Youth a Voice in Politics." Lowell High School, San Francisco, California. See: thelowell.org/opinion/2002-03/mar14-walkout.html, viewed on 3/14/03.
[248] "The National Youth & Student Peace Coalition." See nyspc.net/lobbyday.html viewed on 6/35/03.
[249] President Bush said, "Size of protest -- it's like deciding, well, I'm going to decide policy based upon a focus group." Purdum, Todd. "Focus Groups?" *NYTimes*, 02/23/03 Section 4, p. 5.

opportunity to discuss their lives, culture and politics.[250] We chose to communicate with Iraqi youth because we know from our own experiences on sports teams and at conferences the effect that communication and interaction can have in changing previously conceived attitudes about people. Perhaps youth dialogue can help avert a multi-decade war.

Our biggest fear is how long this war on terrorism will last. Former CIA Director James Woolsey believes the United States is now engaged in World War IV. Woolsey described the Cold War as the Third World War and said this Fourth World War would last us some time. He said the new war is actually against three enemies: "the religious rulers of Iran, the fascists of Iraq and Syria, and Islamic extremists like Osama bin Laden's al Qaeda network."[251] We don't want to live in a world where we learn about new cities by reading which embassy was most recently bombed. Through our nation's soldiers, our diplomats, and perhaps our youth, we want this war to end.

However, we know this war will not end tomorrow. As Millennials we are in this fight for the long run and we know we have the most to lose by inaction overseas and overzealous aggression in foreign lands. Liberals on the left do support our troops, even those who don't march behind the Commander in Chief; conservatives in the generation agree with the President's policy of preemption but are not as enthusiastic about turning their back on international organizations or aspirations for peace. Like all Americans, Millennials hope that peace can be found in the Middle East and do believe we have an important role to play in the conflict and in working for peace.

Since it is members of our generation who are fighting this war, our points of view need to be listened to with more respect. We don't presume to have all the answers to this conflict, but

---

[250] "Bridget to Baghdad: A Youth Dialogue." See: dctvny.org/b2b last viewed on 6/22/03.
[251] Tim Russert on *Meet the Press* (quoting James Woolsey on 04/06/03).

many of us have important questions that need to be asked and answered.

"There is a mysterious cycle in human events ... To some generations much is given. Of other generations much is expected. This generation has a rendezvous with destiny." – *President Franklin Roosevelt*

12

MILLENNIAL STORM

Two thousand four is going to be a very big year. The eldest members of the Millennial Generation will be 28 years old. Our oldest peers will have a chance to run for Congress. Half our generation, forty million of us, will be of voting age, and it will be the first Presidential Election after the Fourth Turning. Turning points in history can rarely be seen so far in advance; are you ready for what's coming? Do you even know what's on the horizon?

In a national survey of the High School Class of 2000, by a two-to-one margin, students "expected to spend more time on politics than Boomers do now. Also by a two-to-one margin, they expect that when they're in charge, government will work better."[252] An April 2002 poll found that "40 percent of young adults aged 18 to 30 say that a career in government is very or fairly appealing to them ... with 54 percent naming helping people or serving the community as the top reasons for service." Whether in government or not, 86 percent of us believe we "have the qualities and character to lead America in the future."[253] The future is now!

---

[252] Howe and Strauss, Millennials Rising, p. 233.
[253] Sitaraman, Ganesh and Previn Warren. Invisible Citizens, p. 84.

In this chapter we review just a small fraction of the many exciting events that will be happening in 2004. Read more and get involved!

March Across America

Mid-June 2004 will mark the beginning of a 3000-mile march from every point of this country to the nation's capital. Over the two-week caravan ending on July 1, 2004, one million Millennials will have taken to the streets. In a massive movement of young people, hitting nearly every major city across the United States, the March Across America will be an opportunity to see your country, converse with other Millennials, and learn about what your government has to offer you. With over 100,000 expected to make it all the way to the Capitol Mall in DC, you can hear the party starting already.

June 14, 2004 will mark the beginning of a 3000-mile journey from every point of this country to the nation's capital. Over the two-week caravan ending on July 1, 2004, thousands, if not millions, of Millennials will have taken to the streets. In a massive movement of young people, hitting nearly every major city across the United States, the March Across America will be an opportunity to see your country, converse with other Millennials, and learn about what your government has to offer you. With thousands expected to make it all the way to the Capitol Mall in DC, you can hear the party starting already.

This March Across America is being organized by Mobilizing America's Youth and dozens of other youth organizations across the country. It was first written about in the fictional book Youth Quake, where a young Seattle band starts a generational revolution ending with a band member running for Congress and one million young people marching on Washington, DC. The March Across America is not a one-day event, but rather a year of planning culminating in two weeks of events, speeches, and concerts. Five different caravans of young people will travel via planes, trains and automobiles to our nation's capital, stopping in cities across the country to have energizing events and rallies. When we march into Washington, blow the horns, and pound the drums of political participation, the walls of the city will certainly come down. This event will define our generation and jumpstart the revolution already underway.[254]

Party Y

While significant, the MYM is not the only event of the year. The first youth party will begin to field candidates for the upcoming election in 2004. Despite being named after a generational misnomer, Party Y is a new independent political party dedicated to meeting the needs of the under-30 population that has the potential and ambition to be a powerful force in our nation's politics. For the last decade there has been a lot of talk about creating a national youth party or even an AARP for young people. After all this talk, the hopes of many young activists are finally coming true. Thomas Bryer is the 24-year-old founder of Reform America, Inc and is one of the core members of the party. Tom identified three goals for the Party Y:

1. Run young people for office
2. Elect more young people to office
3. Increase the percentage of young people voting

This "all-partisan" youth party hopes to embrace the media and hit the road to tap into the political potential of Millennials. With 35 million first time voters as the potential base and the

---

[254] See: m-a-y.org.

reality that only one member of Congress is under thirty (Adam Putnam R-FL), Party Y's leadership is trying to be the necessary catalyst for change. Whether Millennials will actually embrace this new web and media based party remains to be seen. Most importantly, the group will have to prove they can provide a credible voice. But the party has significant potential with many of the all-star, under-thirty activists in this country involved; chances are it will make its mark.

National Youth Conventions

The party platform for Party Y will be created in cooperation with Youth In Action at the National Youth Conventions. In 1996 and 2000, Youth In Action held two youth conventions that were concurrent with the Democratic and Republican National Conventions (however, the events were unaffiliated with any party). At these mirror National Youth Conventions, young people created a National Youth Platform that outlined the issues and political priorities of Millennials across the country. The Platform not only identified top issues, but also proposed solutions to those issues. Once again, young people showed that we can accurately identify problems in our society and generate innovative solutions to problems that have in many cases been around for years.

The National Youth Platform is an instrumental tool in a three-step process that Youth in Action identifies as critical to youth empowerment. According to Youth in Action's organizational goals, youth empowerment occurs when young people have a voice, when that voice can be turned into positive action, and when that action is publicly recognized. To these ends, the Platform provides young people with a national, unified political voice. The Platform is the basis for the Youth Action Guide, which gives young people tips on how to take action on issues in their community. Finally, Youth in Action supports individual activists through the Youth in Action Awards. These $1,000 awards recognize young people who have led innovative projects to create community change. [255]

Goutam Jois, the 21-year old Director of Youth Development for Youth in Action, sums up the organization's goals: "As we head into 2004 and beyond, we know that young people across the country are doing great things in terms of service, have a lot to say about politics, and are involved across demographic lines. We want to provide a forum to amplify Millennials' voices and recognize the incredible work that they are already doing."[256]

The League of Young Voters

Other progressive young leaders in 2003 created the League of Young Voters. While not representing all young voters, this is an important group for young voters left of center. Spearheaded by hip hop activist and author Billy Wimsatt, the mission of this group is to educate young people about candidates and issues and to connect social activists to the political process, especially by voting (bridging the activist gap). Billy is a board member of Rap the Vote and recalls the surprise he felt in 2002 when he went to vote and did not know about all the candidates on the ballot. When well-informed young leaders aren't armed with the adequate, accurate information, it certainly speaks to the disempowerment of your average young voter.

The League of Young Voters has gotten an incredible response from young activists around the country and has three main goals for 2004.

1. Make a progressive voter guide in one city and put it up on the web,

---

[255] Youth In Action Logo. See: youthlink.org.
[256] Jois, Goutam. Interview with Scott Beale. 06/14/03.

2. Create an easy, replicable model for progressive young folks to make local voter guides across the country, and

3. Create a web site to post the voter guides, then print them and use them to mobilize folks to vote.

The League has a progressive bent, but is overall a tool to empower youth. Their themes are education over manipulation, and empowerment through participation.

Conservative Activism

Progressives on the left with the League of Young Voters are not the only ones getting organized. "The Campus Leadership Program has by their own count helped set up 256 conservative campus groups in less than three years. The College Republican National Committee has tripled its membership since 1999 to an all-time high of 1,148 chapters."[257] The Republican National Committee has launched the Excellence in Public Service Series to encourage young conservative women to become more involved in our nation's political process. Strongly organized and generally very well funded, young conservatives are making waves on campuses across the country.

Although not always willing to identify themselves as Republican, many in our generation identify with the traditional values of the Republican party, love the ideology of President Ronald Reagan and have grown up with a "Bush" somewhere on every Republican Presidential ticket except one (in 1996) since birth. The increased liberal activism on college campuses has upset and ultimately inspired many conservatives students to become active. Even on the liberal bastion of the Berkeley campus of the University of California, students rallied in support of the war in Iraq.

The left would be foolish to assume that all young people are either Democratic or apathetic. Before the 2002 election, liberal

---

[257] Colapinto, John. "Armies of the Right: The Young Hipublicans." *NYTimes*, 05/25/03, Section 6, p. 30.

political analyst Stuart Rothenburg was asked at an American University forum "if he thought that eighteen to twenty-four-year olds could be a crucial swing vote in the 2002 election. Rothenberg's sarcastic answer: 'I'm sorry, but you're irrelevant. You don't matter.'"[258] That dominant attitude in the Democratic Party will push more young people to the Republican or Independent Parties. And without a doubt, young conservatives will be key players in the 2004 Republican election strategy and are one more example of the increased political activity of young people today.

Younger Americans Act

As we build into Election Day and politicians increasingly see the power that youth issues and young voters are going to have in the election, momentum will build for the Younger Americans Act. "The Younger Americans Act would create a comprehensive national policy for youth that would ensure that all youth have access to the following core resources: on-going relationships with caring adults; safe places with structured activities; access to services that promote healthy lifestyles; opportunities to acquire marketable skills and competencies; and opportunities for community service and civic participation."[259] The Older Americans Act was passed nearly forty years ago and now all national legislation seemingly favors the elderly. We need comprehensive policy and support for America's young people today.

Youth Vote Coalition

Building up to Election Day, hundreds of youth-run and adult-led organizations will be working to get the vote out. Some will have partisan agendas, others will be seeking success

---

[258] Berkowitz, Jeff. "Democrats have alienated young voters." American University, *The Eagle*, 11/04/02.
[259] *NNYKit*, p. 1.

for certain issues, and many will be trying to increase turnout simply to encourage civic engagement in society, especially among young people. The Youth Vote coalition will be coordinating many of the organizations that are working hard to turnout Millennials on Election Day.

With sites in twelve cities across the country, Youth Vote will be knocking on the doors of young people to register students and turnout youth on Election Day. Their method has been tested and proven effective, and with one hundred member organizations, they reach millions of young people. Although their member and partner organizations are as diverse as Rock the Vote, the Organization for Chinese Americans, Black Youth Vote, the National Council of La Raza, League of Women Voters, the Leadership Institute and even the World Wrestling Entertainment, these diverse groups have come together in a unified effort to rally young voters.

Declare Yourself

In addition to all of these non-profits gearing up for Election Day, Hollywood has declared it is in the mobilization business as well. T.V. Producer Normal Lear has teamed up with Hollywood starts like Drew Barrymore, Ben Stiller, and Vince Vaughn to launch a major campaign to register people to vote. Working with a wide variety of groups including Friendster.com, the National Association of Secretaries of State (NASS), and Newspapers in Education (NIE), *Declare Yourself* will challenge Americans between the ages of eighteen to twenty-nine, especially first-time voters, to find their reason to register and vote. *Declare Yourself* is one more major player that is entering the scene that is building a great deal of momentum towards Election Day.

November 2, 2004

So what does this mean for Election Day?! According to a Harvard study of college students in the spring of 2003, "three in five undergraduates (59%) said they would 'definitely be voting' in the 2004 general election."[260] We predict that Election Day will see an increase in youth turnout, but probably not by more than one to three percent (almost one million more young voters). This won't be because we don't care, but rather because the systemic problems that turn so many young voters off will still be in place in 2004. Furthermore, registration will be a little more difficult on college campuses due to changes in election laws that will have a small negative effect. However, the small increase youth electoral participation will be noticed,

> **Youth Activist Resource: Millennial Politics**
> Millennial Politcs.com is an online resource with lists of hundreds of organizations, more research on activist issues and discussion boards to meet other activists. Go online and find out more at:
> millennialpolitics.com

especially when coupled with the success of events like the March Across America, National Youth Conventions and other activists' events.

There is the story of a young snake named Nate. Slithering through the desert, Nate comes across a lever that says, "If you pull this lever, the world will end." Generations of snakes have passed by this lever and ignored it. When Nate comes by he can see in the distance a large boulder coming down a sand dune, slowly but surely headed towards the lever. Other snakes pass by but Nate decides to stay. The boulder picks up momentum and heads towards the lever – it appears as if the world is surely about to end. Nate stands strong by the lever and at the last minute dives in front of the boulder, ending his life, and

---

[260] *CampusKids.*

bumping it just enough to save the world. The moral of this story is, "Better Nate than Lever."

Currently our political system is in a crash course with the abyss; with each year that passes, our democracy is less legitimate, less democratic, less representative, and less sustainable. Changing the direction of these trends in politics will be very difficult and will require the dedication of many young activists and the participation of us all. However, that is the hard part. Once the direction is changed and more young people begin to participate, more politicians will begin to pay attention. The government will become more responsive and representative, thus leading to greater democracy. The cycle of neglect will be changed to the cycle to resurrect.

After reading eleven chapters it comes down to this: November 2, 2004 will not be a revolution for our generation, but it will be a turning point. The coming Millennial Storm is not going to be as quick as a heat wave that comes and goes with a week of unbearable weather, but then returns to the same average. Nor will the Millennial Storm be as slow as global warming: every few years creeping a degree or two warmer, slowly melting the caps and causing a disruption which none of us can see at one time but know is happening every day. Rather we are in the first few years of a decade-long crescendo of Millennial Generation activism. The activists discussed in this book are trendsetters of youth to come.

The next election will be the end of the preparation for our generation's arrival and the beginning of full participation in the system. It is a crucial date because if we do not turn the train around at that election, even by the smallest of margins, the abyss will be closer than we thought. The rock will be far too near the lever.

Case Study: Mobilizing America's Youth
David Smith was a senior at Berkeley when he became involved in a student lobby day in Sacramento where they successfully lobbied the state legislature on issues important to youth such as student housing, tuition, and the University budget. This experience prompted him to create a national organization to get more young people involved all over the country. In the spring of 2003 they had their first national conference in Washington with young people from across the country coming discuss the political priorities of the generation. Now they are planning the March Across America for the summer of 2004. They story of how David became active is shared by many young activists. When you experience a little bit of success, you can then see how possible it is to make a difference. This feeling of political efficacy is a critical motivator to truly Mobilize America's Youth.

Youth Activism Step #12
Follow Through &
Change the World
If David had been content to successfully lobby Sacramento without following his dream to empower the generation, he would have missed his opportunity to change the world. He has taken a lot of risks, but he does not regret it for a minute.

The Future

We cannot be sure what the future holds, but we are certain that our generation will be the one that shapes it. As sixteen-year-old Sarita Mahtani said in the Seattle Times, "We're not cynical and we don't think it's impossible to do what other previous generations didn't do."[261] This isn't idle talk of a teenager; it is an announcement of things to come.

The best way to understand the future is to study the past. Generational scholars William Strauss and Neil Howe present a compelling argument for how cycles in American history have

---

[261] Mahtani, Sarita. "We're Ready to Shape the World." The Seattle Times, 07/31/97. See: seattletimes.com/extra/browse/html97/math_073197.html

created a civic generation with today's Millennials. We have every reason to believe our generation will be like that of our grandparents who fought in World War II or the Revolutionary figures who founded this country. We have issues to address, we have begun to get involved, and we have the potential to shape the world. Now we just need to make it happen.

We are entering a new age. Just as the Industrial Revolution changed the world a century ago, today the Information Revolution and the Internet are propelling us into a new age. In this new era, people are more open to trying things in different ways. This openness to new policy, to new technology, and to new ideas will allow business leaders, scientists and policy makers to be more creative in their work and less constrained by path dependency. New ideas will be free to evolve more quickly than before, and once combined with the current Communications Revolution, these ideas will spread faster and be more readily accepted.

So what does this mean practically? It means that Millennials will be less constrained in the workforce. Politicians will be able to lead with political courage, business leaders can do what they think is best for the business and best for the community, and scientists will be given even greater latitude to explore, investigate and invent. This combination of hope for the future and personal self-confidence will make society as a whole less risk-adverse. This is the zeitgeist of our generation, the spirit of our era.

A Lucky Generation

People are not inherently different from one age to the next. Millennials are not innately better or worse than the Boomers or Gen Xers, but because different opportunities are available and different challenges exist for today's youngest generation, a large cohort of the population is growing up with a deep concern for others and an ability to act on this concern in countless different ways.

Gen Xers were unlucky – they were born and came of age in a time that did not invest in their future or provide them a lot of chances. Boomers told them they were worthless, and they were not given many opportunities to prove their parents wrong. Eventually they believed the lies they were told. Boomers selfishly held on to their positions of power and a generation that grew up in hard times was unable to make something of themselves. Despite tech entrepreneurs and amazing service leaders, with no serious war to motivate patriotic soldiers and enrage young pacifists, a generation grew up unable to shake the label of slacker.

In contrast, today Millennial youth are entering the workforce and they are taking society by storm. Knowledge and ease of the use of computers and technology set this generation apart. Access to information and self-confidence will educate and empower today's youngest population cohort. And finally, our generation will succeed thanks to the support and encouragement from the older segment of the population that is finally looking to the young to address some of the ills of society.

Millennials will lead the youth revolution that will usher in an exciting period in American History. Our generation has incredible potential. Edward Winter of The U30 Group sees the future of this generation: "Think of them [Millennials] as this quiet little group about to change everything." David Bositis from the Joint Center is optimistic too. According to his understated analysis, "young adults appear to be more civic-minded than might be expected – encouragingly so – and in many ways more so than Generation X."[262] Elizabeth Large of the *Baltimore Sun* agrees. "We think (the Millennials) are a

---

[262] *DivGen*, p. 45.

revolution in the waiting. When they do revolt against the system, there's going to be a consensus (with the Boomers) as to which direction the change should move."[263]

Out of our generation will come the Presidents, civic role models, and world leaders who will define this century. The entelechy, or full potential of the generation, and the spirit of the age offers great promise for the United States; and if vigilance towards moral goals is victorious over complacency, then the next one hundred years of America's future will indeed be very bright. If this can happen, then Millennials will be the most influential generation in the 21st century, just like the G.I. generation was the most influential in the 20th.

The Choice Ahead of Us

There is no historic inevitability that we will be the next greatest generation; there is no such thing as manifest destiny. While we have no guarantee of grandeur, we will definitely have the opportunity to change the world and a choice for how we will do it. We have no excuses. We've been given all the tools we need and despite the shortcomings of our parents and mistakes made by society, we stand on the shoulders of giants.

So now is the time. People may tell you to wait. "They will say that you *are too young* to change this world: But don't ever listen to them… Remember… Lafayette was 19 when he came to America to help us win the Revolutionary War. Martin Luther King Jr. was too young to run for President when he won the Nobel Peace Prize, and Jesus Christ would have barely qualified for the U.S. Senate the day he was crucified at 33."[264]

This book is a call to arms to get involved and to motivate others. But now it is up to you. You've read some success stories and have been given a road map to achieve your own goals. Somehow this book got into your hands and you must get

---

[263] Large, Elizabeth. "The Millennials." *Baltimore Sun*, 1/24/99, p. D1.
[264] Clayton, Zach. High School Valedictory Address, 05/31/03.

it into the hands of someone else. You've forwarded thousands of meaningless emails; it is time to pass on something that actually matters. Give this to a friend and debate where we missed the mark; tell ten friends to buy the book and learn what issues your peers care about; get a dozen people to read the book and see how your community begins to change. It is a real shame that more people don't know about all the opportunities out there and the issues facing us – it is a much bigger shame when you do learn what's going down and choose to do nothing about it.

No matter what your political ideology;
No matter what your ethnic, racial, or religious background;
No matter what your age, economic class, or educational level;
And, no matter how cynical you were before today.

We need you to be the difference this country needs;
We need you to inspire others to get involved;
We need to all work together, as a generation;
And, only then will we create a better world.

"Be the change you want to see in the world."
– Gandhi

APPENDIX

"An invasion of armies can be resisted,
but not an idea whose time has come." – *Victor Hugo*

THE MANIFESTO[265]

We are America's future. We are a generation ready to take on the world. We believe our parents have failed to take into account the future or our values in today's politics. ⚅ We believe in **individual responsibility**; and as individuals we must be able to work with others for a common good. ⚅ We believe that **community service** is an important form of youth activism, but that politics, business, and faith are still necessary to improve our country. ⚅ We believe that every being is affected when **the environment** is polluted. We demand greater responsibility from corporations, communities, the government, and individuals for addressing environmental problems. Environmental protection should neither be a hobby of the wealthy nor a burden of the poor; it is a global problem that we all must address. ⚅ Respect for **human rights** for all people is essential to the strength of any society, including a global one. ⚅ We are a generation that sees the positive potential of **internationalism** – the exchange of people, cultures, and economic ties that bind countries. ⚅ We also see the potential pitfalls of **globalization** if supranational companies, governments and organizations are not held accountable for maintaining environmental protection, upholding labor standards, or addressing local needs. ⚅ Our generation has strong faith and **religion** is important to us. This spiritual base is at the root of

---

[265] Quotes from this document come from the 2001 Century Institute's Sagner Fellows as well as official youth statements at dozens of non-partisan conferences.

much of our activism. ⚡ We believe the war on **drugs**, the war on **crime**, and current **gun** policies need to be re-examined and modified with a new voice. ⚡ During our lifetimes, crime has dropped and yet the **prison industrial complex** has grown. ⚡ We demand urgent action to address **growing inequality.** The psychological, physical, and political implications of economic inequality are not given their due attention. ⚡ Our *most* important political priority is **education**. As the sum total of all school age children in America, we see how some schools are failing and the cost of higher education is rising. Education must be locally administered but federally supported. ⚡ We believe that **racism and discrimination** still exist in our country and must be ended before they tear apart the unity of our nation. Our generation will end racism. ⚡ **Voting** is important to us. Many in our generation are fighting to lower the voting age. In fact, there is a new civil rights movement in our generation for **youth rights.** We do not believe that it is acceptable to discriminate against people for any reason, including age. We also value **human life.** A majority of us think both the death penalty and abortion should be legal and more rare. ⚡We believe in **liberty**. The government has an important, but limited, role to play in society. ⚡ We are concerned about **terrorism** and the expanding **wars** overseas. The defense of our country is paramount to us, but so too are the values that make our country great. We are not a monolithic block, but we all agree that there are many things wrong with this world **and we all have a responsibility to stand up and fight for a better tomorrow.**

"Far better it is to dare mighty things, to win glorious triumphs, even though checkered by failure, than to take rank with those poor spirits who neither enjoy much nor suffer much, because they live in the gray twilight that knows not victory nor defeat." – *President Theodore Roosevelt*[266]

TWELVE STEPS TO YOUTH ACTIVISM

Inspirational books, educational texts, and motivational speeches are worthless changeagents unless they illuminate a clear path to action. From our combined experiences with youth activism, we hope the following twelve steps serve as a useful roadmap to making the transition from getting upset about an issue to changing the world.

Below we have summarized each of the Twelve Steps that are included in each chapter. We hope you enjoyed the examples of youth activists who are using these twelve steps as well as the organizations in each chapter that are our there to help you become a successful young activist. Now it is your turn! Follow these steps and you will be on your way.

1. Find an Issue that Upsets You

You wake up one morning and find the world is somehow different to you. You realize that you can no longer sit by and passively participate in life, especially when there is so much that we need to fix. Mastering video games, going to band camp, and playing soccer are no longer fulfilling your mission in life. It is time for you to take action. So, what are you passionate about? Getting upset is the first step to becoming an activist! You cannot stop there though; you have a ways to go...

---

[266] Roosevelt, Theodore, speech before the Hamilton Club, Chicago, 04/10/1899.

2. Educate Yourself

We are the most educated generation in the history of the world. We have access to more information than the Rhodes Scholars of previous generations; all we need to do is tap into it and be able to comprehend it. After you've identified an issue you care about, the next step is to learn the various sides of the argument. Read, listen, argue, absorb, become an expert on the issue you care about and never stop learning about it. However, beware of the "perfect information" argument – you can never know everything about an issue. At some point, you must take your knowledge, your gut instinct, your faith, and the courage of your convictions and go to step number three ...

3. Take Action

A. *Join a Group*

Now it is time to get involved. Is there a group out there addressing the issue you care about? If so, then get involved, get your feet wet, and learn the ropes of effecting social change. Try out different kinds of activism through the group and you'll learn the ropes. The rest of these twelve steps will be informative to you, but even more so for those of you who are planning to ...

B. *Start a New Organization*

Perhaps the issue you care about is not being addressed by anyone else. For instance, you care about drug testing, but no one is organizing in your high school. In that case, it is time to start a new group. These next steps will certainly help ...

4. Find Your Vision

How will the world look when you've changed it? You know what upsets you, and you've gotten started, but where are you headed? Draft your mission statement. Define what success means to you. What are your personal (and organizational) goals? How will you make your mark? How will you evaluate your progress? Don't forget this important step, then ...

5. Recruit Your Friends

Tell everyone about your vision – your friends, family, possible allies, and even complete strangers. As you give voice to your vision, you will recruit the necessary support to be successful. Some people will disagree, others will even fight against you, but with some effort you can find hundreds, and then thousands, who care. Remember what Margaret Mead taught us: "Never doubt that a small group of thoughtful, committed citizens can change the world. Indeed, it is the only thing that ever has."[267] Embrace her optimism, and take her 'group' emphasis to heart...

6. Get Organized

Once you have the leadership of your team, you've got to get organized. Have your first meeting, set out a timeline, create a budget, detail your needs, write your strategic plan, and delegate responsibilities to accomplish your goal. Changing the world will take a lot of work, so you'd better get organized ...

7. Build a Coalition

Think back to step number three. Were there organizations that you considered joining before you launched your own group? Go back to those organizations and build a strong coalition to achieve a common goal. Always network, since there are organizations, adults, and other Millennials who share your vision. Collaborate rather than compete to achieve success together, then ...

8. Invite the Public and Press on Board

Use your age to your advantage. At first, people may not take you seriously, but you will get noticed because you are a "youth activist." Be professional and persuasive. Get the press – even your school paper – on board with your cause. Create blogs and collect emails for your e-newsletter. Put meetings times on an

---

[267] Mead, Margaret. See: brainyquote.com/quotes/quotes/m/q100502.html.

online calendar. You have an interesting story that should be told. It is now time to ...

9. Hold an Event

You've done the legwork, and now it's time for your first major event. Lead a sit-in, launch your website, start a boycott, make a speech, begin a dialogue, promote a fundraiser, hold a news conference, stage a walkout, and get everyone involved. You've been working toward this day; so make it as successful as possible! Be sure to also ...

10. Maintain Momentum

Remember that your guiding goal is not an event, but a movement – so keep moving! You should have already planned what the next event will be, so announce it at your big event. Be sure to also meet with your team after your kick-off to evaluate the first event. Learn from your mistakes and then get back out there. Know when to push forward and when to regroup. There is more work to do ...

11. Develop a Community of Support

Start surrounding yourself with other activists, including people working on other issues. These will be friends who will support you personally and keep you motivated and inspired even after months on a campaign or years fighting for social justice. This community is different than a coalition that is project- or goal-oriented. This is to keep you, as a person, going strong. A solid community of support will make it a lot easier to keep going and avoid burnout...

12. Follow Through and Change the World.

World-changing youth activists are not sprinters; they are marathon runners. So follow up and follow through. Stay committed to your cause and keep advancing to the next stage.

Include young members in your group to pass on leadership. Connect your volunteerism to your activism and your activism to your politics. Serve your community, fight for justice, and vote your conscious. Keep an eye on the prize and be ready to accept that you're in it for the long run. Success can be slow and incremental, but still gratifying and effective. Luckily you are young, so you have a lifetime to achieve your goals!

Take These Twelve Steps To Youth Venture

What do Michelle Chen, Billy Hallowell, Ian Carter, Laura Lockwood, Kenny Wiggins, Dan Freilich, Nina Sung, Robin Chen Delos, and David Smith all have in common? Not only are they profiled in Millennial Manifesto, but also they are supported by Youth Venture.

Thousands of young activists across the country have turned to Youth Venture to receive assistance to turn their ideas into reality. If you are twenty or younger and want up to $1,000 to launch your civic-minded organization, club, or business, then all you need to do is go to www.youthventure.org and fill out your application!

The requirements are simple. You must have a team of young people who are starting something new and sustainable that makes a difference in the community. You must have a credible plan and budget, and an older ally to support your work. Your venture *must* be youth-led, and it can deal with almost *any* issue.

In addition to receiving up to $1,000 to launch your project, Youth Venture will provide workshops, tools, special opportunities, and access to an online network of young activists. Youth Venture wants to change the way society looks at young people by supporting young people who are doing amazing things. *What do YOU want to do to make your world a better place?*

"It's great to know that youth have the right to change their own worlds, but I'm almost 18. It seems like by the time youth recognize their power, they are too old to be a part of the youth movement any longer." – *Jill Peters, California Coalition for Youth*

HOW TO GET INVOLVED

It is time to stop sitting on the sidelines and complaining about how life is passing you by. It is time to stop waiting for someone to do something when you are the very person that needs to get involved. It is time to become a part of MillennialPolitics.com.

MillennialPolitics.com is not a membership based organization, a special interest, or a youth political action committee. We do not want to recreate the wheel and dilute our generational power any more than it already is. Millennial Politics is committed to educating and motivating people about youth activism and generational politics. We do three things: 1) Share information; 2) Organize events; and 3) Network activists. We share information through this book, our website, our newsletter, and online discussion boards. We organize events through our speakers bureau, book clubs, coffee and politics groups and by co-sponsoring activities. Finally, we network activists with these tools and more. Ultimately, we believe there is value in creating a generational identity that enables us to change our country and shift the current elder-focused political paradigm.

If you want to join a national coalition of diverse organizations to promote youth civic engagement, join Youth Vote. If you want to become a social entrepreneur and meet other Millennials who are starting businesses or organizations to change their communities, then become a Youth Venturer. If you want to bridge the "service gap," then check out United Leaders. Those interested in volunteerism should check out Youth Service America. Find a non-profit job at Idealist.org. Raise money for youth activism with the 2100 Fund. If you want to be part of the March Across America, join up with Mobilizing America's Youth. Get involved with Youth In Action to help write the next National Youth Platform. There are hundreds of great groups out there and you can find most of them in this book and on MillennialPolitics.com. Check out our website, join the network, invite a speaker to your campus, and get involved.

Please do it today. We are asking for you to help. Together we can build a better tomorrow for our country. Thanks for your support!

– Scott Beale, Abeer Abdalla and everyone with Team Millennial

How To Start a
Millennial Politics Book Club

If you liked this book so much that you are reading every page of the Appendix, then you need to start a Millennial Politics Book Club. Millennial Politics book clubs are for people of all ages. We have more information online – at millennialpolitics.com/bookclubs – but here are the basics.

1) **Find People.** Get together some friends and classmates. Put an add in the local free paper. Send out an email to people who might be interested. Tell them you are starting a Millennial Politics book club where you are going to read books about youth activism and politics, especially ones by young authors.

2) **Order More Books.** Millennial Manifesto is available for one-third off the cover price if you buy ten books or more. So get at least ten people on board.

3) **Set A Date.** Give people about a month to read each book. Find a date, like the first Wednesday night of every month, where everyone agrees to come together.

4) **Prepare Questions.** We have sample questions online for each chapter of <u>Millennial Manifesto</u> to help facilitate conversation.

5) **Meet, Discuss, and Debate.** When you finally get together, discuss what you liked and didn't like, what you agree with and what you think is crazy.

6) **Continue the Conversation.** Go online and be sure to let us know what you think of the book. Use our discussion boards to meet other readers. Talk about it in school, at work and on the bus.

7) **Choose the Next Book.** We have suggestions for ten books to get you started, but do not limit yourself to our choices. Generally it is a good idea to pick books two months in advance. Additionally, you can almost always get discounts with group orders.

8) **Start Coffee and Politics.** Meet once a month to discuss the book, and then once more just to get together and talk politics. Bring in speakers, debate current events, and meet other people like you who want to affect social change.

9) **Turn Talk Into Action.** As you learn more about these social issues, turn your book club into an activist group. Participate in political events, organize service projects, and connect what you are reading to the outside world. If you are twenty or younger, go to youthventure.org for support.

10) **Recruit More People.** Tell your friends in other schools in other cities to get involved. Just imagine what we could all achieve.

BOOKCROSSING, 2100 FUND, AND MORE

BookCross Millennial Manifesto!

BookCrossing is one of the largest reading groups on the web, and as far as we can tell the largest free book club in the world. The way it works is after you read a book, you then register it online and "release it into the wild." Eventually someone will find the book, and hopefully go to bookcrossing.com and say where they found the book and what they think of it. We love the idea of BookCrossing and want to encourage our readers to use this as a promotional tool so *Millennial Manifesto* can be read by as many people as possible. Here is what we propose:

If you loved this book, then help us make sure everyone knows about it. Register the book on bookcrossing.com and place it in a place where other people will be sure to pick it up, like near a school or in a coffee shop. It is also a great idea to release copies of *Millennial Manifesto* near radio stations, local newspapers and other media outlets. Maybe near City Hall or your professor's office. Be sure to leave a note letting them know that the book is free and to check out this page. Then, please come back to MillennialPolitics.com and buy another copy of *Millennial Manifesto* for your own library. If you release a book into the wild, then be sure to let us know and your next book will be 25% off the cover price. Learn more at: www.millennialpolitics.com/bookcrossing.

2100 Fund: How To Throw Parties For Charity

One great way you can get involved in your community is by throwing a party for charity. If you are interested in doing this, check out the 2100 Fund. The 2100 Fund is a nonprofit organization started by Scott Beale that raises money for youth activist and cancer fighting charities by throwing large parties.

The formula is quite simple. If you are over twenty-one, then get a group of friends together who want to have a party at a bar, restaurant, club or some other venue. Negotiate with the venue for a deal, usually free space in return for a promised amount of revenue. The next step is to invite tons of people and collect a nominal cover charge at the door. If you chose to work with the 2100 Fund, then half of the money goes to a cancer or youth activist non-profit, and the other half goes to build an endowment to support these charities in the long run. If you are not twenty-one, then you may still organize a 2100 Fund party, obviously, just not with alcohol. To find our more about how to get involved with the 2100 Fund, check out www.2100fund.org.

What is the Fourth Turning? (from fourthturning.com)

The Fourth Turning is a concept and a book by William Strauss and Neil Howe. Published in 1997, Strauss and Howe predict in this book that just after the millennium, America will enter a new era that will culminate with a crisis comparable to the American Revolution, the Civil War, the Great Depression, or World War II. Strauss and Howe base this vision on a provocative theory of American history as a series of recurring 80- to 100-year cycles. Each cycle has four "turnings"- a High, an Awakening, an Unraveling, and a Crisis. In the book, the authors locate today's America as midway through an Unraveling, roughly a decade away from the next Crisis (or Fourth Turning). However, since the book was published Strauss and Howe believe that September 11th was the start of the Fourth Turning.

To fully appreciate some of the generational concepts in this book, it is highly recommended that you at least check out fourthturning.com or better yet, buy the book, <u>The Fourth Turning.</u>

SOURCES

Given the vast range of topics covered in this book – and the innumerable scholarly, journalistic, and pop culture sources that relate to these issues – there is no way everything can be referenced. We tried to include as many footnotes as possible, but as a convenience, a brief list of sources is provided below.

Readers particularly interested in generational theory and characteristics of Millennials are strongly encouraged to read the many relevant books published by William Strauss and Neil Howe.

Here are the full citations for references that were abbreviated in the footnotes.

Text References

Abbreviations

2000 NYP	2000 National Youth Platform Foundation of America: Youth in Action
ABCampaigns	Alliance for Better Campaigns
AP	Associated Press
CampusKids	Schneiders / Della Volpe / Schulman, "Campus Kids: The New Swing Voter." Harvard University, Institute of Politics Spring Survey, 5/21/03.
Census	U.S. Bureau of the Census
CDC	Centers for Disease Control and Prevention
ChiTrib	The Chicago Tribune
CIRCLE	Center for Information and Research on Civic Learning and Engagement. The University of Maryland School of Public Affairs. www.civicyouth.org
DivGen	"Diverging Generations." Bositis, David. Washington, DC: Joint Center for Political and Economic Studies, 2000.
Future500	Future 500. Active Element Foundation. New Orleans: Subway & Elevated Press, 2002. p. 3.

Gallup	Gallup Poll News Service, The Gallup Organization. www.gallup.org
KFFSurvey	Kaiser Family Foundation. "New Survey Shows Most Young Adults have Strong Opinions on Top Campaign Issues, But Many Still Not Planning to Vote." Press Release 09/25/00. kff.org/content/2000/3058/PressRelease.PDF
LATimes	The Los Angeles Times
Millennials2College	Howe and Strauss, <u>Millennials Go To College</u>, New York: Life Course Associates, 2003. p. 24.
NASSMillennium	National Association of Secretaries of State. "New Millennium Project Part I: American Youth Attitudes on Politics, Citizenship, Government and Voting." 10/2/99 www.stateofthevote.org
NatYouthSurvey2000	Raducha, Peter. "Preliminary Results of a Nationwide Survey of Youth." Oregon State University: The Program for Governmental Research and Education, 07/00. oregonstate.edu/dept/pol_sci/pgre/gyan.htm
NCES	National Center for Education Statistics, See: nces.ed.gov
NewStudentPolitics	"The New Student Politics." Long, Sarah, et al. Campus Compact, Providence, RI, 2002. p. 20.
NYPost	New York Post
NYT	The New York Times
NNYKit	Hughes, Della, Miriam Rollin and Cassandra McKee, "2001 Advocacy Kit." Washington, DC, National Network for Youth, 2001. p. JJDPA-5.
Project540	"Project 540: Students Turn for A Change" Kelly, Angela, ed. 2002, Providence College.
Reuters	Reuters News Service
Salon	Salon.com Magazine
SF Chronicle	The San Francisco Chronicle
Time	Time Magazine
TrustMatters	Trust Matters, "Is Anyone Listening." An Issue Report from the Partnership for Trust in Government. N. 1, Spring 2002. See: youngcitizensurvey.org.
UCLA/HERI	L.J. Saxs, A. W. Astin, W. S. Korn, and K.M. Mahoney, The American Freshman (Higher Education Research Institute, University of California at Los Angeles), published annually since 1966.

UCLA/HERI30yr	Astin, Alexander, et al, <u>The American Freshman:</u> <u>Thirty Year Trends.</u> Los Angeles, Higher Education Research Institute, 1997.
USNews	U.S. News and World Report
WashPost	The Washington Post

Books

Bagby, Meredith. <u>We've Got Issues.</u> New York: Public Affairs, 2000.

Behr, Gregg et al. <u>The Content of Our Character.</u> Durham, NC: Kenan Ethics Program, 1999. *See: contentofourcharacter.org.*

Boyers, Sara Jane. <u>Teen Power Politics.</u> Brookfield, CT: The Millbrook Press, 2000.

Cherny, Andrei. <u>The Next Deal.</u> New York: Basic Books, 2001.

Clayton, Zach, et. al. <u>Freedom's Answer.</u> Washington, DC: Freedom's Answer Foundation, 2003. *See: freedomsanswer.com.*

Lesko, Wendy. <u>Youth! The 26% Solution.</u> New York: infoUSA, Inc, 1999.

Lobel, Paul Rogat. <u>Soul of a Citizen.</u> New York: St. Martin's Press, 1999.

Males, Mike. <u>Framing Youth,</u> Monroe, Maine: Common Courage Press, 1999.

Sam, Cousin. <u>Youth Quake.</u> Victoria, Canada: Trafford, 2002.

Schneider, Barbara and David Stevenson. <u>Ambitious Generation.</u> New Haven: Yale University, 1999.

Sitaraman, Ganesh and Previn Warren. <u>Invisible Citizens.</u> New York: iUniverse, Inc., 2003.

Strauss and Howe. <u>Generations.</u> New York: William Morrow and Company, 1991.

<u>The Fourth Turning.</u> New York: Broadway Books, 1997. *See: fourthturning.com.*

<u>Millennials Rising.</u> New York: Vintage Books, 2000.

<u>Millennials Go To College.</u> New York: Life Course Associates, 2003

Tapscott, Don. <u>Growing Up Digital.</u> New York: McGraw-Hill, 1998.

Wimsatt, William. <u>No More Prisons.</u> Chicago: Soft Skull Press, 1999.

Websites

afj.org	The Alliance for Justice.
arsalyn.org	Arsalyn Foundation
bettercampaigns.org	Alliance for Better Campaigns
booksnotbars.org	Books Not Bars
campaignyoungvoters.org	Campaign for Young Voters
ChannelOne.com	Channel One Television
closeup.org	Close Up

dol.gov	Department of Labor
fairvote.org	Center for Voting and Democracy
fbi.gov	FBI Uniform Crime Reports, 2001.
freechild.org	The Freechild Project
freedomsanswer.org	Freedoms Answer
heartofamerica.org	Heart of America Foundation
hrc.org	Human Rights Campaign
lisn.org	Listen, Inc.
m-a-y.org	Mobilizing America's Youth
nces.ed.gov	National Center for Education Statistics
numbersUSA.com	Numbers USA (Immigration info)
nylc.org	National Youth Leadership Council
peacefire.org	Peace Fire
pirg.org	Public Interest Research Group
presidentialclassroom.org	Presidential Classroom
rockthevote.org	Rock the Vote
takingitglobal.org	Taking it Global
teenpowerpolitics.com	Teen Power Politics
unitedleaders.org	United Leaders
usstudents.org	United States Student Association
voteforamerica.org	Vote for America
whatkidscando.org	What Kids Can Do
whitehousedrugpolicy.gov	White House Office of National Drug Control Policy
youngcitizensurvey.org	"Key Findings on Opportunities for Candidates: What are Youth Looking For?" Center for Democracy and Citizenship.
youthactivism.com	Youth Activism Project
youthvote.org	Youth Vote
youthlink.org	Youth In Action and the Global Youth Action Network
youthnoise.com	YouthNOISE
youthrights.org	National Youth Rights Association (NYRA)
youthventure.org	Youth Venture
ysa.org	Youth Service America

For more information about everything you have read about as well as an extensive list of books, organizations and websites, please go to
w w w . m i l l e n n i a l p o l i t i c s . c o m

INDEX

The Index has been broken down into seven different categories for your convenience: Colleges & Universities, Corporations, Issues, Media, Organizations, People, and Regional Activism.

"Few will have the greatness to bend history itself; but each of us can
work to change a small portion of events, and in the total of all those
acts will be written the history of this generation."
— *Senator Robert F. Kennedy*

HOW IN THE WORLD
DID THIS BOOK GET PUBLISHED &
ACKNOWLEDGMENTS

This book has been in the works for about six years. Scott
Beale began it when he was a student at Georgetown in
December of 1997 when Professor Charles King approached him
about writing a book about Generation X. Six years later it is
now the <u>Millennial Manifesto</u> that is in your hands.

Publishing a book is hard. Publishers, agents, and others in
the industry would kindly consider the idea for months before
telling us no. Countless other authors offered to help but without
much luck. Our conclusion – publishers did not want to print a
positive book about young people; they did not think there were
enough active young people to buy a book like this; and, they did
not want to empower our generation with this tool. In a very
Millennial way, we have self-published this book. So help us by
spreading the word. Proclaim out loud the power of our
generation – together we will work to empower our generation to
fight for a better world! You may not agree with everything we
write, but hopefully you agree with our mission.

If it had not been for the encouragement and support of
thousands of people, this book would never have been
completed. If it had not been for the work of hundreds of young
activists, this book would be no good. If it had not been for you
reading these words, then the book would have been worthless.
Please pass this book on to others (or encourage them to buy it!)
and contact us with questions or comments.

Since over 100 people contributed to this book and
supported Millennial Politics over the year, please go to

millennialpolitics.com/acknowledgments to read the full list of supporters and why we love these people so much. We owe a particular debt of thanks to Professor Charles King for starting the project, Bill Strauss for being a mentor over the years, D.A. Wallach for giving up a summer to intern with an unemployed struggling author because he believed in the cause, and Clint Schaff for being the number one volunteer and motivator. We would also particularly like to thank the following people for their 100+ hour commitment to this project: Everyone involved with the MillenniumKids group, Anne Beale, Courtney Kramer, Mark Waner, David Smith, Mary Anne Beale, Sahar Abdalla, Tiffany Eberle, Michelle Macon, Sara Mooney, Alayna Smith, Maritza Valenzuela, Allan Shore, Amanda Fuhr Maurer, Goutam Jois, Ian Carter, Billy Hallowell, Vikram Raghavan, Erin Ross, Jesse Levey, Meredith Lobel, Danielle Brown, Zach Clayton, Howard Thomas, Ben Quinto, Jamie Zembruski, Andy Berman, Alex Koroknay-Palicz, Thad Ferber, Carolyn Darrow, Samuel Thomas, Ryan Goldman, Adam Stellato, Becky Hale, Alex Piper, Tracy Mann, and many more who we regret to have forgotten but have certainly put online.

We would also like to thank the following other authors who gave us support along the way: Bill Strauss, Billy Wimsatt, Neil Howe, Wendy Lesko, Abby Wilner, Danny Seo, Sara Jane Boyers, and Jesse Vickey.

Finally, we would both like to thank our families who are a constant source of support and inspiration.

ABOUT THE AUTHORS

Scott Beale

Scott is a recognized leader of the Millennial Generation with an impressive record of political activism and public service. He is currently the Mid Atlantic Director for Youth Venture, a national nonprofit that promotes youth social entrepreneurship, and a regular speaker about youth activism. For ten years he has been an advocate for his generation.

As a freshman at Georgetown, Scott organized rallies at the U.S. Capitol to protest cuts in federal financial aid. These rallies generated so much attention that over 500 students from six local colleges and universities attended as well as numerous Administration and Congressional speakers. He later authored The Pledge for Community Service, a document Georgetown students embraced as a guide to community action. Scott's own volunteer work during college included registering voters with Rock the Vote, taking him to both the New Hampshire primaries, and the Democratic National Convention. By the end of Scott's senior year, his leadership on campus won him the recognition of the University President and campus papers, which labeled him one of "the most prominent students on campus." Additionally, Scott was nominated for the school's highest honor, the Spronk Medal.

Since college, Scott's activism has extended beyond the United States, three times taking him to Bosnia, once as the youngest member of an advance U.S. State Department group. While there, he became the youngest core supervisor from any country for the Organization for Security and Cooperation in Europe (OSCE), an intergovernmental organization responsible for supervising elections in war-recovering Bosnia. Scott's management of a forty-five person international team resulted in the successful registration of over 30,000 Bosnian voters. In the States, Scott has worked as a Legislative Assistant for Delaware Governor Tom Carper, former Chair of the National Governors' Association, and as the Associate Director of Intergovernmental Affairs in the Clinton White House.

In addition to his political life, for over five years, Scott has been researching, writing and speaking about the Millennial Generation. He helped best-selling authors William Strauss and Neil Howe with their book on the generation, *Millennials Rising*; and, he is part of the Leadership Circle of United Leaders, a youth political organization based out of Harvard University. He is also a columnist for the Politix Group and a contributing writer to Adam Magazine. Scott has given over 100 speeches on the political attitudes and activism of the generation at conferences, on college campuses, in high schools, in the United States Capitol, and in the White House. He has even appeared on CBS's the Early Show talking about the generation. Established in 1998, his website, MillennialPolitics.com (and its earlier versions) has been a constant source of activist information for youth.

In addition to promoting youth activism through Millennial Politics, for the last two years Scott has contributed to the 300% growth of Youth Venture and their support of youth activists nationwide. He is also the founder of the 2100 Fund, a non-profit that organizes events to raise money for charity. He recently began his Masters in Public Administration at the University of Delaware.

Abeer Abdalla

After a nationwide search in which over 200 young political leaders applied, Abeer Abdalla was selected by Scott Beale to be the contributing author of <u>Millennial Manifesto</u>. As a Republican, an Arab-American, a Muslim, and a younger woman, she balances Scott's point of view in many ways and brings to the book an impressive record of advocating for Millennials.

A graduate of the Islamic Saudi Academy in Mt. Vernon, Virginia, Abeer holds dual-diplomas certifying both a formal education in Arabic Language and Islamic Studies from The Royal Kingdom of Saudi Arabia Ministry of Education as well as a U.S. high school accredited education. While in college in Boston, MA she founded the College Republicans on her campus and was elected class president. She is currently on sabbatical in the quest to further pursue her commitment to youth activism.

Abeer has a history of remarkable achievement for such a young American. During her high-school years she was an active participant in the Model United Nations program, winning numerous awards including Best Delegation and Most Outstanding Representation. Concurrently, Abeer founded and was Editor-in-Chief of the Academy bilingual newspaper for four years. Participating in the Presidential Classroom Scholars Program she met U.S. Representative Tom Davis (R-VA) and subsequently got involved with his re-election campaign.

Since then, Abeer has volunteered for the Massachusetts Republican State Committee and played more significant roles as Volunteer Coordinator of the grassroots Jack Robinson for U.S. Senate Campaign, Director of Operations for The Massachusetts Citizens Alliance and Executive Director of The Parent's Rights Coalition. During the 2000 Presidential election, Abeer played an active role as a volunteer for Bush for President, as Regional Campaign Coordinator for Service Vote 2000, and advocate for Youth Vote 2000. Currently, Abeer is an active member of the Arab-American Institute, The League of Women Voters, Pioneers of Change, The National Rifle Association, the Republican National Committee, The Young Republicans, and the National Federation of Republican Women. Through her commitment to education, Abeer has worked with numerous high school and college Model United Nations, Political Science and International clubs to further their knowledge of our nation's place in today's increasingly global society. She is a featured activist, as Ms. September, in the Youth Leadership Initiative's 2003-2004 calendar.

Abeer is a passionate leader of the Millennial Generation and has written several articles about politics and youth involvement. She is a contributing columnist for the former youth-charged web site, PowerStudents.com, current columnist for the Bull Moose Republicans and the Politix Group. Abeer has debated and spoken many times on our generation's politics, most recently about Homeland Security at the Lou Frey Symposium in Orlando, Florida.

This book is not meant to be the final word on the generation.
Keep the conversation going!
w w w . m i l l e n n i a l p o l i t i c s . c o m

MORE PRAISE FOR MILLENNIAL MANIFESTO & MILLENNIAL POLITICS.COM

"I was fortunate to meet Scott and some of his team this summer in Washington. They are intelligent, driven, and thoughtful. Our generation needs a voice and Scott is doing a great job! As Scott is a former employee of [the Clinton Administration] and I am an ardent Republican campaign worker, I thought we might disagree, but Scott is extremely persuasive and comes across as a genuine leader of the new political generation."
– Fritz Brogan, *National Chairman Teenagers For Republican Victory* [268]

"Scott Beale is truly visionary. Mobilizing 'Millennials' is very challenging, but in utilizing the web, Beale harnessed the power of online community to inspire young activists. MillennialPolitics.com is a really vibrant online community that hosts much debate and discussion about issues pertinent to youth activists. … Kudos to Scott and Abeer!"
– Debbie Castro, *Washington, DC*

"Scott and Abeer are modeling a formula for change for this generation: collaboration. Millennial Politics is finding ways to recognize activism on a variety of topics from a plurality of voices. It could be a cacophony. But, somehow, Millennial Politics has shown that all that noise really does have a forward motion. I look forward to seeing what the Millennial Team can accomplish. Scott is clearly amazing at getting this done. This project has taken off in only a couple years!"
– Cristina Aquino, *South Bend, Indiana*

"I am inspired by Millennial Politics' extraordinary potential to motivate and organize young people, and am impressed by the extent to which Scott has already done so. I am 18, and have also noticed the need to involve, inform, and engage young Americans to make a difference in the world and accomplish outstanding feats."
– Dan Freilich, *Chevy Chase, Maryland*

---

[268] Freilich, Aquino, Castro, and Brogan quotes about Scott Beale and Millennial Politics appeared in FastCompany.com: fastcompany.com/fast50/profile/index.html?beale202.

READ THIS BOOK!

"Our generation has no excuse not to be engaged and work for social change. As you are about to read, there are too many pressing issues that demand the creative, capable hands, and minds of the Millennial Generation. We must not sit idly by and listen to the band play on as our nation sinks unable to overcome partisan rhetoric and a public turned off to our failing democracy. We will not be passive participants in our nation's politics; it is time for us to make ourselves be heard!"
— *Scott Beale and Abeer Abdalla*

CRITICAL PRAISE FOR MILLENNIAL MANIFESTO & MILLENNIAL POLITICS.COM

"Focusing on the REAL concerns, strengths, intelligence, and activism of today's key generation, in Millennial Manifesto, Scott and Abeer provide a backdrop, the script, and set the stage for a dramatic revolution taking place that is bringing new energy and positive change into our democracy."
— Sara Jane Boyers, Author, *Teen Power Politics*

"Youth activists are shaking up the political world, whether by opposing globalization or fighting to lower the voting age, they are working for causes that appeal to them. Scott Beale and Abeer Abdalla have written a great Manifesto that outlines these issues for this emerging political generation. The authors care, interest, and direct involvement with the political life of the Millennial Generation is genuine. They have sought input from all corners of society. This is an excellent book for anyone seeking to dispel negative notions about youth, and see the empowered individuals they really are. This book shows that Millennials aren't slackers, but citizens seeking empowerment."
— Alex Koroknay-Palicz, President, *National .Youth Rights Association*